LLM Engineering

A Practical Guide to Designing, Deploying, and Scaling Large Language Models for Real-World AI Applications

Charles Sprinter

Copyright Page

LLM Engineering: A Practical Guide to Designing, Deploying, and Scaling Large Language Models for Real-World AI Applications

Disclaimer

The information provided in this book is for educational purposes only. While every effort has been made to ensure the accuracy of the content, the author and publisher make no representations or warranties regarding the completeness, reliability, or suitability of the information. The use of the information in this book is at the reader's own discretion and risk.

All trademarks, service marks, product names, and logos appearing in this book are the property of their respective owners. The use of such marks is not intended to imply any affiliation with or endorsement by their owners.

Table of contenet

Introduction

1. Welcome to the World of LLMs

1.1 What Are Large Language Models?

Large Language Models (LLMs) are advanced artificial intelligence systems designed to understand and generate human-like text. They are powered by deep learning architectures, typically based on transformers, and trained on vast amounts of text data. LLMs analyze patterns in language to perform tasks such as answering questions, generating text, translating languages, and more.

Key features of LLMs:

- Scale: LLMs are characterized by their size, measured in the number of parameters (e.g., GPT-3 has 175 billion parameters). These parameters allow the model to capture intricate details of language and context.

- General-Purpose Utility: They can perform a wide variety of tasks, such as summarization, sentiment analysis, and even programming assistance, often without task-specific fine-tuning.

- Learning Capabilities: LLMs can adapt to new tasks with minimal additional training through techniques like fine-tuning and prompt engineering.

1.2 Importance of LLMs in Modern AI Systems

LLMs represent a significant breakthrough in AI due to their ability to process and generate text that feels natural and contextually appropriate. They have transformed the way AI interacts with humans and are the foundation for numerous real-world applications. Below are some reasons why LLMs are pivotal in modern AI systems:

1. Improved Understanding of Natural Language:
   - LLMs excel at understanding the nuances of human language, including slang, idioms, and varying tones, enabling better communication between humans and machines.

2. Versatility Across Domains:
   - These models are not limited to specific tasks. For example:
     - Healthcare: Assisting doctors by summarizing patient data.
     - Customer Support: Powering chatbots for faster resolution of customer queries.

- Education: Personalizing learning experiences for students.

3. Accessibility to AI Solutions:

   o Pretrained LLMs (e.g., GPT, BERT) available via open-source platforms like Hugging Face have democratized access to advanced AI, enabling developers and researchers to build AI applications without training models from scratch.

4. Efficiency and Automation:

   o LLMs streamline operations, reduce human error, and enable automation in complex workflows such as document summarization, content generation, and coding.

1.3 How LLMs Are Transforming Industries (Real-World Examples)

LLMs are revolutionizing numerous industries by providing powerful tools for automation, decision-making, and innovation. Here are examples of how LLMs are making an impact:

1. Healthcare

- Application: Patient Record Summarization

- How It Works: LLMs can process unstructured data (e.g., doctors' notes, medical reports) and summarize key details, improving efficiency in patient care.

- Example Tool: MedPaLM, a healthcare-specific adaptation of GPT models.

2. Finance

- Application: Fraud Detection

- How It Works: By analyzing transaction patterns and text descriptions, LLMs help detect fraudulent activities in real-time.

- Example Tool: BERT-based solutions for analyzing financial reports.

3. Customer Support

- Application: Intelligent Chatbots

- How It Works: LLMs power virtual assistants that understand and respond to customer queries effectively.

- Example Tool: ChatGPT by OpenAI, widely used for automating customer interactions.

4. Education

- Application: Personalized Learning
- How It Works: LLMs analyze a student's learning style and provide tailored recommendations for improvement.
- Example Tool: GPT-4-based tutors for generating quizzes and personalized study plans.

1.4 What You Will Learn in This Book

This book is a comprehensive guide to mastering LLM engineering, covering everything from the basics to deploying and scaling real-world applications. Here's a roadmap of what you'll learn:

Foundational Concepts

- The architecture of LLMs: Transformers, attention mechanisms, and tokenization.
- Key terminologies like embeddings, positional encoding, and pretraining.

Designing and Training LLMs

- How to prepare data and customize models for specific tasks.
- Fine-tuning pretrained models to improve performance on domain-specific datasets.

Deployment and Optimization

- Building inference pipelines for real-time applications.
- Scaling LLMs to handle large user bases while optimizing cost and performance.

Real-World Applications

- Practical projects, including chatbot development, text summarization, and sentiment analysis.
- Case studies showcasing how LLMs solve real-world problems across industries.

Emerging Trends

- Exploring multimodal models (text, image, audio integration).
- Understanding techniques for building smaller, efficient models like LoRA (Low-Rank Adaptation).

By the end of this book, you'll have the knowledge and skills to confidently build, deploy, and scale LLMs for diverse applications.

1.5 How to Use This Book Effectively: Code, Exercises, and Projects

This book is designed to be hands-on and interactive. To maximize your learning, follow these tips:

1. Follow the Code Examples

- Each chapter includes fully functional, annotated code examples to demonstrate concepts.

- Example: Installing Hugging Face Transformers:

python

```
# Install the transformers library
!pip install transformers

# Import a pretrained model and tokenizer
from transformers import AutoModelForCausalLM, AutoTokenizer

model_name = "gpt2"
tokenizer = AutoTokenizer.from_pretrained(model_name)
model = AutoModelForCausalLM.from_pretrained(model_name)

# Tokenize input text
input_text = "What is the capital of France?"
input_ids = tokenizer(input_text, return_tensors="pt").input_ids

# Generate a response
output = model.generate(input_ids, max_length=50,
num_return_sequences=1)
print(tokenizer.decode(output[0], skip_special_tokens=True))
```

2. Complete the Exercises

- Exercises at the end of each chapter provide hands-on practice to reinforce your understanding. Example:

    o *"Experiment with different tokenization techniques (WordPiece vs. Byte Pair Encoding) and compare the results."*

3. Build the Projects

- Larger projects guide you through real-world implementations, such as:

    o Deploying a chatbot with GPT and Flask.

    o Creating a summarization tool for news articles.

4. Leverage Visual Aids

- Diagrams and flowcharts clarify complex concepts, such as the transformer architecture and distributed training setups.

5. Use the GitHub Repository

- Access all code, datasets, and solutions in the accompanying GitHub repository. This will allow you to focus on learning rather than setup.

In this introduction, you've gained a brief overview of what large language models are, why they're transformative, and how they're impacting industries. You've also learned what to expect from this book and how to make the most of it. With this foundation, you're ready to dive into the exciting world of LLM engineering!

2. Setting the Stage

In this chapter, we'll lay the foundation for understanding Large Language Models (LLMs) by exploring their history, foundational concepts, and the tools necessary to work with them. By the end of this chapter, you will have a clear understanding of how language models evolved, the core concepts underpinning LLMs, and the tools you need to start building and testing these models.

2.1 A Brief History of Language Models: From N-Grams to Transformers

The evolution of language models has been marked by a series of milestones, each building on the advancements of the previous generation. Here's an overview of this journey:

1. Early Statistical Models

- **N-Grams**:
  Early language models used statistical methods to predict the next word in a sequence based on the last N words.

  - For example, in a bigram model ($N = 2$), the probability of a word depends only on the previous word

$$P(wn|wn-1) = \frac{count(wn-1,wn)}{count(wn-1)}$$

  - **Limitations**:
    - Cannot capture long-term dependencies.
    - Fixed vocabulary leads to poor generalization.

2. Introduction of Neural Networks

- **Feedforward Neural Networks**:
  Neural networks introduced embeddings, where words are represented as dense vectors capturing semantic meaning.

    o However, these models still struggled with context over long sequences.

- **Recurrent Neural Networks (RNNs)**:
  RNNs introduced sequential processing, allowing models to learn dependencies across time steps.

    o **Limitations**: Struggled with long-term dependencies due to vanishing gradients.

3. The Breakthrough of Transformers

- **Transformer Models** (2017):
  The introduction of the Transformer architecture by Vaswani et al. in the paper *"Attention Is All You Need"* revolutionized natural language processing (NLP).

    o **Key Features**:

        ▪ **Self-Attention**: Focuses on different parts of the input sequence to capture context effectively.

        ▪ **Parallel Processing**: Unlike RNNs, transformers process entire sequences simultaneously, enabling faster training.

    o Models like **GPT** and **BERT** are based on this architecture.

2.2 Key Concepts: Tokens, Embeddings, Attention, and Pretraining

Understanding the foundational concepts is essential to working with LLMs effectively. Let's break down each of these ideas.

1. Tokens

- **Definition**: Tokens are the smallest units of text processed by a model, such as words, subwords, or characters.

    o For example, the sentence *"I love coding"* might be tokenized as:

        ▪ Word-level: [I, love, coding]

        ▪ Subword-level: [I, lov, ##e, coding]

        ▪ Character-level: [I, , l, o, v, e, , c, o, d, i, n, g]

- **Why Tokenization Matters**:

      ○ It balances vocabulary size and flexibility. Sub word tokenization (e.g., Byte Pair Encoding, WordPiece) is commonly used in modern models.

2. Embeddings

- **Definition**: Embeddings map tokens to dense vector spaces, where semantically similar words have similar representations.

  ○ Example: Words like *king* and *queen* will have embeddings close to each other in the vector space.

- **Importance**:

  ○ Embeddings allow models to understand the relationships between words, phrases, and contexts.

3. Attention Mechanisms

- **Analogy**: Think of attention as a spotlight focusing on the most relevant parts of a sentence.

  ○ Example: In the sentence *"The cat sat on the mat,"* attention helps the model understand that *"cat"* is the subject.

- **How It Works**:

  ○ Attention assigns weights to different parts of the input sequence, helping the model prioritize important information.

4. Pretraining and Fine-Tuning

- **Pretraining**:
  Models are trained on large, generic datasets to understand language broadly.

  ○ Example: GPT models are pretrained on vast amounts of internet text.

- **Fine-Tuning**:
  The pretrained model is then fine-tuned on a smaller, task-specific dataset to adapt to specific use cases (e.g., sentiment analysis, summarization).

2.3 Tools of the Trade: PyTorch, TensorFlow, Hugging Face, and More

1. PyTorch

- A popular deep learning library known for its flexibility and ease of use.

- **Strengths**:

  ○ Dynamic computation graphs.

  ○ Extensive community support.

- Example Use Case: Training custom models or fine-tuning transformers.

2. TensorFlow

- A widely used library for deep learning, known for scalability.
- **Strengths**:
  - Static computation graphs (suitable for production).
  - Integration with TensorFlow Serving for deployment.

3. Hugging Face Transformers

- Hugging Face provides pretrained models, datasets, and tokenizers that make working with LLMs easier.
- **Why Hugging Face?**
  - Pretrained models like BERT, GPT, and T5 are available.
  - High-level APIs for tasks like text classification and generation.

Code Example: Installing and Setting Up Hugging Face Transformers

python

```python
# Install the Transformers library
!pip install transformers

# Import a pretrained model and tokenizer
from transformers import AutoTokenizer,
AutoModelForSequenceClassification

# Load a tokenizer and model for sentiment analysis
tokenizer = AutoTokenizer.from_pretrained("bert-base-uncased")
model = AutoModelForSequenceClassification.from_pretrained("bert-base-
uncased")

# Tokenize a sample sentence
inputs = tokenizer("I love natural language processing!",
return_tensors="pt")

# Perform inference
outputs = model(**inputs)
print(outputs.logits)  # Logits for sentiment classification
```

Exercise : Load and Test a Small Language Model Using Hugging Face

1. **Objective**: Load a pretrained model and test its basic functionality.

2. **Steps**:

    o Install the Hugging Face library.

    o Load the distilbert-base-uncased model.

    o Tokenize a sample sentence and perform inference.

3. **Solution**:

python

```
from transformers import AutoTokenizer,
AutoModelForSequenceClassification

# Load a smaller, efficient model
tokenizer = AutoTokenizer.from_pretrained("distilbert-base-uncased")
model =
AutoModelForSequenceClassification.from_pretrained("distilbert-base-
uncased")

# Tokenize input
text = "This book is fantastic!"
inputs = tokenizer(text, return_tensors="pt")

# Perform inference
outputs = model(**inputs)
print(outputs.logits)
```

Summary

- Language models have evolved from simple statistical approaches to advanced Transformer architectures.

- Core concepts like tokens, embeddings, attention mechanisms, and pretraining are the building blocks of LLMs.

- Tools like PyTorch, TensorFlow, and Hugging Face make it easier to work with modern LLMs.

By mastering these foundational ideas and tools, you're now equipped to dive deeper into the world of LLM engineering. In the next chapter, we'll explore how to design LLMs tailored for specific tasks.

Chapter 1: Foundations of Large Language Models

Learning Objectives

By the end of this chapter, you will:

1. Understand what makes a language model "large."

2. Learn about the key components of large language models, including transformers and attention mechanisms.

3. Explore foundational innovations like self-attention and positional encoding that enable scalability.

4. Implement a basic attention mechanism in Python.

1.1 Understanding the Basics

1.1.1 What Makes an LLM "Large"?

A **Large Language Model (LLM)** is a neural network trained on vast datasets and designed to generate or process natural language. But what exactly makes it "large"?

Key Factors:

1. **Number of Parameters**:

   o Parameters are the model's learned weights during training.

   o Modern LLMs like GPT-3 can have **hundreds of billions of parameters**, enabling them to learn and generalize complex patterns in language.

   o Example:

     ▪ GPT-3 has ~175 billion parameters.

     ▪ By contrast, GPT-2 has ~1.5 billion parameters.

2. **Size of Training Data**:

   o LLMs are trained on diverse, massive datasets, including books, websites, and other text sources.

   o Example: OpenAI trained GPT models on datasets containing hundreds of gigabytes of text data.

3. **Context Window**:

- The number of tokens the model can process in one forward pass.
- Larger context windows allow LLMs to understand long-term dependencies in text.
- Example: GPT-3 can process up to 2048 tokens, while GPT-4 can handle even more.

4. **Computational Resources**:
   - LLMs require powerful GPUs/TPUs and significant memory for training and inference.

1.1.2 Anatomy of an LLM: Transformers, Attention, and Beyond

At the core of an LLM is the **Transformer architecture**, introduced in the groundbreaking paper *"Attention Is All You Need"* (Vaswani et al., 2017). Here's how it works:

1. Transformer Architecture Overview

- **Key Components**:
  - **Encoder**: Processes the input sequence (e.g., for translation tasks).
  - **Decoder**: Generates the output sequence.
  - Modern LLMs like GPT use only the decoder, while BERT uses only the encoder.

2. The Flow of Data in a Transformer

1. Input text is **tokenized** into smaller units (tokens).
2. Tokens are converted into **embeddings** (dense vector representations).
3. Embeddings are processed through **multi-head self-attention layers**, capturing relationships between tokens.
4. The output is passed through **feedforward neural networks** to refine it.
5. Layers are repeated multiple times to build deeper representations.

1.1.3 Key Innovations: Self-Attention, Positional Encoding, and Scalability

1. Self-Attention
Self-attention enables the model to focus on relevant parts of the input sequence.

- **Analogy**: Imagine reading a book. While reading a paragraph, your brain focuses on certain words or sentences that clarify the context.

- **How It Works**:
  - Each word (token) attends to every other word in the sequence.
  - Attention scores are calculated using three vectors:
    - **Query (Q)**: Represents the token asking for information.
    - **Key (K)**: Represents the tokens providing information.
    - **Value (V)**: Represents the actual information.

$$Attention(Q,K,V) = softmax(\frac{QKT}{\sqrt{d_k}}) \ \mathbf{v}$$

2. Positional Encoding

Transformers process input sequences simultaneously, losing token order.

- **Solution**: Add **positional encodings** to embeddings to retain order information.

- **Equation for Positional Encoding**:

$$PE(pos,2i) = \sin\left(\frac{pos}{100002i/dmodel}\right)$$

$$PE(pos,2i+1) = \cos\left(\frac{pos}{100002i/dmodel}\right)$$

3. Scalability

Transformers scale efficiently because they process sequences in parallel, unlike Recurrent Neural Networks (RNNs), which process sequentially.

Examples: Diagrams to Illustrate Attention Mechanisms

Diagram: Self-Attention in a Sentence

Consider the sentence *"The cat sat on the mat."*

Token	Query Vector (Q)	Key Vector (K)	Attention Weight
The	Focuses on "cat"	Relates to "sat"	High for "cat"
Cat	Focuses on "sat"	Relates to "on"	High for "sat"

- Visualization: The attention layer would show a heatmap where weights indicate relevance

---

Code: Visualizing a Simplified Transformer Layer Using PyTorch

python

```python
import torch
import torch.nn as nn

# Define self-attention layer
class SelfAttention(nn.Module):
    def __init__(self, embed_size, heads):
        super(SelfAttention, self).__init__()
        self.embed_size = embed_size
        self.heads = heads
        self.values = nn.Linear(embed_size, embed_size, bias=False)
        self.keys = nn.Linear(embed_size, embed_size, bias=False)
        self.queries = nn.Linear(embed_size, embed_size, bias=False)
        self.fc_out = nn.Linear(embed_size, embed_size)

    def forward(self, values, keys, query):
        attention = torch.einsum("nqhd,nkhd->nhqk", [query, keys])
        attention = torch.nn.functional.softmax(attention, dim=-1)
        out = torch.einsum("nhql,nlhd->nqhd", [attention, values])
        return self.fc_out(out)

# Example use
embed_size = 256  # Embedding size
heads = 8         # Number of attention heads
seq_len = 10      # Length of input sequence
batch_size = 2    # Number of sequences in a batch

# Dummy data
values = torch.rand((batch_size, seq_len, embed_size))
keys = torch.rand((batch_size, seq_len, embed_size))
queries = torch.rand((batch_size, seq_len, embed_size))

attention = SelfAttention(embed_size, heads)
output = attention(values, keys, queries)
print("Output Shape:", output.shape)
```

Output:
The code outputs a transformed tensor, ready for subsequent processing layers.

Exercise : Implement a Basic Attention Mechanism in Python

1. **Objective**: Implement and test a basic attention mechanism.

2. **Steps**:

    ○ Create query, key, and value tensors.

    ○ Calculate attention weights.

    ○ Compute weighted sums of values.

3. **Solution**:

python

```
import numpy as np

# Initialize Query, Key, and Value matrices
query = np.array([1, 0, 1])   # Example query vector
key = np.array([[1, 0, 1], [0, 1, 0], [1, 1, 0]])   # Keys matrix
value = np.array([[10, 0], [0, 10], [5, 5]])   # Values matrix

# Compute attention scores
scores = np.dot(query, key.T)
weights = np.exp(scores) / np.sum(np.exp(scores), axis=0)   # Softmax

# Compute weighted values
output = np.dot(weights, value)
print("Attention Output:", output)
```

Summary

1. **LLMs are "large"** due to their parameter size, training data, and computational requirements.

2. **Transformers** introduced revolutionary concepts like self-attention and positional encoding, enabling scalability and performance.

3. With basic code examples, you've visualized a transformer and implemented a basic attention mechanism.

You're now ready to explore the practical design of LLMs in the next chapter!

1.2 Core Components of LLMs

Understanding the core components of Large Language Models (LLMs) is essential to grasp how they process text and perform tasks. These components work together to transform raw input text into meaningful outputs.

1.2.1 Input Tokenization and Embeddings

What is Tokenization?

Tokenization is the process of splitting raw text into smaller units (tokens) that the model can process. These tokens could represent:

- Words: *"I love coding"* → ["I", "love", "coding"]

- Subwords: *"coding"* → ["cod", "##ing"]

- Characters: *"coding"* → ["c", "o", "d", "i", "n", "g"]

Modern models like BERT and GPT use **subword tokenization** (e.g., WordPiece, Byte Pair Encoding) to balance vocabulary size and generalization.

Why Tokenization Matters

Tokenization ensures that:

- Models can handle out-of-vocabulary (OOV) words by breaking them into subwords.

- Memory usage is optimized by limiting vocabulary size.

What are Embeddings?

Once text is tokenized, each token is mapped to a dense vector representation called an **embedding**. These embeddings capture the semantic meaning of tokens in a way that numerically represents their relationships.

- Example:

  - Tokens like *"king"* and *"queen"* will have embeddings that are close in the vector space because of their semantic similarity.

Code Example: Tokenizing Text and Extracting Embeddings with Hugging Face

python

```python
# Import the necessary modules
from transformers import AutoTokenizer, AutoModel

# Load a pretrained tokenizer and model
tokenizer = AutoTokenizer.from_pretrained("bert-base-uncased")
model = AutoModel.from_pretrained("bert-base-uncased")

# Input text
text = "I love natural language processing."

# Tokenize the input text
inputs = tokenizer(text, return_tensors="pt")

# Extract embeddings
with torch.no_grad():  # No gradient computation needed for inference
    outputs = model(**inputs)
    embeddings = outputs.last_hidden_state

# Print the shape of embeddings
print("Embeddings shape:", embeddings.shape)
```

Output:
For an input sequence of length n, the shape of embeddings will be:

(Batch Size, Sequence Length, Embedding Dimension)\text{(Batch Size, Sequence Length, Embedding Dimension)}(Batch Size, Sequence Length, Embedding Dimension)

Example:

Embeddings shape: (1, 8, 768)(Batch of 1, 8 tokens, 768 dimensions per token).\text{Embeddings shape: (1, 8, 768)} \text{(Batch of 1, 8 tokens, 768 dimensions per token)}.Embeddings shape: (1, 8, 768)(Batch of 1, 8 tokens, 768 dimensions per token).

Exercise : Experiment with Different Tokenizers

Objective: Understand how different tokenizers (e.g., WordPiece, Byte Pair Encoding) split text.

Steps:

1. Use Hugging Face's tokenizers for bert-base-uncased (WordPiece) and gpt2 (Byte Pair Encoding).

2. Compare the tokenization results for the same input sentence.

Solution:

python

```
# Load tokenizers for different models
bert_tokenizer = AutoTokenizer.from_pretrained("bert-base-uncased")  #
WordPiece
gpt_tokenizer = AutoTokenizer.from_pretrained("gpt2")  # Byte Pair
Encoding


# Input text
text = "Tokenization is important for LLMs."

# Tokenize with both tokenizers
bert_tokens = bert_tokenizer.tokenize(text)
gpt_tokens = gpt_tokenizer.tokenize(text)

print("WordPiece Tokens:", bert_tokens)
print("Byte Pair Encoding Tokens:", gpt_tokens)
```

Output:

less

WordPiece Tokens: ['token', '##ization', 'is', 'important', 'for', 'll', '##ms', '.']

Byte Pair Encoding Tokens: ['Token', 'ization', 'Ġis', 'Ġimportant', 'Ġfor', 'ĠLL', 'Ms', '.']

1.2.2 The Encoder-Decoder Paradigm: How It Works

The **encoder-decoder paradigm** is a key architecture in natural language processing tasks such as machine translation, summarization, and text-to-text generation.

Encoder

The encoder processes the input sequence and generates a fixed-length vector representation (context).

- Example: Input sentence *"The cat sat on the mat."*

Decoder

The decoder uses the encoder's output to generate the target sequence token by token.

- Example: Output translation in French: *"Le chat s'est assis sur le tapis."*

How It Works in Practice

1. **Encoder**: Processes input tokens and encodes their relationships.
2. **Decoder**: Decodes the representation step by step, using:
   - **Self-Attention**: Focuses on the generated output so far.
   - **Encoder-Decoder Attention**: Focuses on the encoder's representation.

Example: Real-World Applications

- **Machine Translation**:
  - Input: *"Hello, how are you?"*
  - Output: *"Bonjour, comment ça va ?"*
- **Summarization**:
  - Input: Long document.
  - Output: Concise summary.

1.2.3 Feedforward Networks, Multi-Head Attention, and Layer Norm

These components form the building blocks of transformers.

1. Feedforward Networks

- Transform embeddings after attention to capture deeper patterns.

   Equation $Output = ReLU(W1 \cdot Input + b1) \cdot W2 + b2$

- Feedforward layers are applied independently to each token.

2. Multi-Head Attention

Allows the model to focus on multiple aspects of the input simultaneously by using multiple attention heads.

- **How It Works**:

  - Split embeddings into smaller subspaces for each head.

  - Perform self-attention in parallel for each head.

  - Concatenate the results and pass them through a linear layer.

3. Layer Normalization (Layer Norm)

Layer Norm stabilizes the training process by normalizing the inputs to each layer.

- **How It Works**:

  - Normalize the input features: $Norm(x) = \dfrac{x - \mu}{\sqrt{\sigma 2 + \epsilon}}$

Code Example: Multi-Head Attention Implementation in PyTorch

python

```python
import torch
import torch.nn as nn

class MultiHeadAttention(nn.Module):
    def __init__(self, embed_size, heads):
        super(MultiHeadAttention, self).__init__()
        self.embed_size = embed_size
        self.heads = heads
        self.head_dim = embed_size // heads

        assert (
            self.head_dim * heads == embed_size
        ), "Embedding size must be divisible by heads"
```

```python
        self.values = nn.Linear(self.head_dim, self.head_dim,
bias=False)
        self.keys = nn.Linear(self.head_dim, self.head_dim,
bias=False)
        self.queries = nn.Linear(self.head_dim, self.head_dim,
bias=False)
        self.fc_out = nn.Linear(embed_size, embed_size)

    def forward(self, values, keys, query):
        N = query.shape[0]
        value_len, key_len, query_len = values.shape[1],
keys.shape[1], query.shape[1]

        # Split the embedding into self.heads different pieces
        values = values.reshape(N, value_len, self.heads,
self.head_dim)
        keys = keys.reshape(N, key_len, self.heads, self.head_dim)
        queries = query.reshape(N, query_len, self.heads,
self.head_dim)

        energy = torch.einsum("nqhd,nkhd->nhqk", [queries, keys])  #
Queries * Keys
        attention = torch.softmax(energy / (self.embed_size ** (1 /
2)), dim=3)

        out = torch.einsum("nhql,nlhd->nqhd", [attention,
values]).reshape(
            N, query_len, self.embed_size
        )

        return self.fc_out(out)

# Testing the Multi-Head Attention
embed_size = 256
heads = 8
seq_length = 10
batch_size = 2

values = torch.rand((batch_size, seq_length, embed_size))
keys = torch.rand((batch_size, seq_length, embed_size))
queries = torch.rand((batch_size, seq_length, embed_size))

attention = MultiHeadAttention(embed_size, heads)
output = attention(values, keys, queries)
print("Output Shape:", output.shape)
```

Output:

Output Shape: (2, 10, 256)(Batch Size, Sequence Length, Embedding Size).\text{Output Shape: (2, 10, 256)} \text{(Batch Size, Sequence Length, Embedding Size)}.Output Shape: (2, 10, 256)(Batch Size, Sequence Length, Embedding Size).

Summary

- **Tokenization and embeddings** convert text into a format LLMs can process.
- The **encoder-decoder paradigm** enables models to handle complex tasks like translation.
- Key components like **feedforward networks**, **multi-head attention**, and **layer normalization** form the backbone of transformers.

With this knowledge, you are now prepared to understand training and fine-tuning in upcoming chapters.

1.3 LLM Families and Use Cases

Understanding the families of Large Language Models (LLMs) and their use cases is key to selecting the right model for a given task. This section explores the most popular models, compares open-source and proprietary options, and demonstrates real-world applications.

1.3.1 Overview of Popular Models: GPT, BERT, T5, LLaMA, etc.

Over the years, several LLM families have emerged, each with unique strengths and specialized use cases.

1. GPT (Generative Pretrained Transformer)

- **Developer**: OpenAI
- **Architecture**: Decoder-only transformer focused on generating coherent and contextually relevant text.
- **Key Features**:
  - Trained on massive datasets with causal language modeling (predicting the next word based on previous words).
  - Capable of long-form text generation, summarization, and conversation.
- **Popular Versions**:
  - GPT-2: Open-source with 1.5 billion parameters.

- GPT-3: Proprietary with 175 billion parameters, supports zero-shot and few-shot learning.

- GPT-4: Enhanced context understanding and multimodal capabilities.

- **Use Cases**:

  - Chatbots: Virtual assistants like ChatGPT.

  - Text generation: Blog posts, stories, code snippets.

---

2. BERT (Bidirectional Encoder Representations from Transformers)

- **Developer**: Google AI

- **Architecture**: Encoder-only transformer designed for understanding context by looking at both directions (bidirectional).

- **Key Features**:

  - Pretrained using masked language modeling (predicting masked words in a sentence) and next sentence prediction.

  - Highly effective for text classification, question answering, and sentiment analysis.

- **Popular Versions**:

  - BERT (base and large): Open-source, widely adopted.

  - RoBERTa: A robustly optimized variant of BERT.

- **Use Cases**:

  - Question answering: Systems like Google Search.

  - Sentiment analysis: Analyzing customer reviews.

---

3. T5 (Text-to-Text Transfer Transformer)

- **Developer**: Google Research

- **Architecture**: Encoder-decoder transformer designed to convert all NLP tasks into a text-to-text format.

- **Key Features**:

  - A unified framework where input and output are always text.

  - Simplifies tasks like translation, summarization, and classification.

- **Popular Versions**:
  - T5 (base, large): Open-source and customizable.
- **Use Cases**:
  - Summarization: Condensing articles into shorter texts.
  - Translation: Converting text between languages.

4. LLaMA (Large Language Model Meta AI)

- **Developer**: Meta AI
- **Architecture**: Decoder-only model focused on efficiency and performance.
- **Key Features**:
  - Scales effectively with fewer resources compared to GPT-3.
  - Primarily designed for research and open applications.
- **Popular Versions**:
  - LLaMA 1: Compact yet powerful.
  - LLaMA 2: Enhanced capabilities and openly available.
- **Use Cases**:
  - Research-focused NLP tasks.
  - Educational applications in natural language understanding.

Comparison Table of Popular Models

Model	Developer	Architecture	Primary Use Case	Open-Source?
GPT	OpenAI	Decoder-only	Text generation, chatbots	Partially
BERT	Google AI	Encoder-only	Context understanding, QA	Yes
T5	Google Research	Encoder-decoder	Summarization, translation	Yes
LLaMA	Meta AI	Decoder-only	Research, efficient applications	Yes

1.3.2 Open-Source vs. Proprietary Models: Pros and Cons

Choosing between open-source and proprietary LLMs depends on the project's requirements, budget, and ethical considerations.

Open-Source Models

Examples: BERT, T5, LLaMA

- **Pros**:
    - Free to use: No licensing costs.
    - Customizable: Can be fine-tuned for specific tasks.
    - Transparent: Community-driven improvements and audits.
- **Cons**:
    - Resource-intensive: Requires significant compute power for training and fine-tuning.
    - Limited Support: Relies on community forums for troubleshooting.

Proprietary Models

Examples: GPT-3, GPT-4 (OpenAI), Claude (Anthropic)

- **Pros**:
    - Pretrained and optimized: Ready-to-use for various tasks.
    - Scalability: Managed by providers with powerful infrastructure.
    - Dedicated Support: Comes with technical support and SLAs.
- **Cons**:
    - Expensive: High usage costs, especially for large-scale applications.
    - Black-box nature: Limited transparency in training and data.

Use Cases of LLMs in Real-World Scenarios

1. **GPT (Chatbots)**:
    - GPT powers chatbots like ChatGPT, providing conversational AI for customer service, education, and virtual assistants.
    - Example Prompt:

- **Input**: "Explain quantum mechanics in simple terms."
- **Output**: "Quantum mechanics studies the behavior of very small particles, like atoms and electrons. It's like a set of rules for the tiny building blocks of our universe."

2. **BERT (Question Answering)**:

   o Example: Implementing a FAQ system where users query a database for specific answers.

   - **Input**: "What is the capital of France?"
   - **Output**: "The capital of France is Paris."

3. **T5 (Summarization)**:

   o Example: Summarizing news articles.

   - **Input**: Full article about climate change.
   - **Output**: "Climate change is accelerating, requiring urgent action globally."

4. **LLaMA (Research)**:

   o Example: Developing efficient NLP models for academic research.

Exercise : Explore Outputs from Different Models on Hugging Face Hub

Objective: Compare the outputs of BERT, GPT-3, and T5 for the same input.

Steps:

1. Use Hugging Face Transformers to load three models: BERT (question answering), GPT-2 (generation), and T5 (summarization).

2. Input the same text and observe the differences.

Solution:

python

```
from transformers import pipeline

# Load models
qa_model = pipeline("question-answering", model="bert-large-uncased-whole-word-masking-finetuned-squad")
generation_model = pipeline("text-generation", model="gpt2")
summarization_model = pipeline("summarization", model="t5-small")
```

```
# Input text
text = "Hugging Face is a company that specializes in natural language
processing. It has open-source tools for developers."

# Question Answering with BERT
qa_output = qa_model(question="What does Hugging Face specialize in?",
context=text)
print("BERT QA Output:", qa_output['answer'])

# Text Generation with GPT-2
generation_output = generation_model("Hugging Face is", max_length=20,
num_return_sequences=1)
print("GPT-2 Generation Output:",
generation_output[0]['generated_text'])

# Summarization with T5
summarization_output = summarization_model(text, max_length=30,
min_length=5, do_sample=False)
print("T5 Summarization Output:",
summarization_output[0]['summary_text'])
```
Expected Outputs:

- **BERT QA Output**: "natural language processing"

- **GPT-2 Generation Output**: "Hugging Face is a great platform for building applications."

- **T5 Summarization Output**: "Hugging Face specializes in NLP and provides open-source tools."

Summary

1. **LLM Families**:

    o GPT excels in generation and conversational AI.

    o BERT is ideal for understanding context in text.

    o T5 simplifies diverse NLP tasks using a text-to-text framework.

    o LLaMA focuses on efficiency and research applications.

2. **Open-Source vs. Proprietary**:

    o Open-source models offer flexibility but require resources.

    o Proprietary models are ready-to-use but come at a cost.

3. **Real-World Applications**:

- LLMs power chatbots, question answering systems, summarization tools, and more.

This knowledge prepares you to select and implement the right LLM for your projects. In the next chapter, we'll dive into designing LLMs for specific use cases.

Chapter 2: Designing Large Language Models

Learning Objectives

By the end of this chapter, you will:

1. Understand how to balance model size, complexity, and performance when designing LLMs.

2. Learn how to assess dataset requirements, address trade-offs, and curate data for training effective LLMs.

2.1 Key Design Principles

When designing a Large Language Model (LLM), careful planning is essential to ensure the model meets the desired performance, scalability, and efficiency goals. This section explores two critical principles: balancing model size, complexity, and performance, and managing dataset requirements and trade-offs.

2.1.1 Balancing Model Size, Complexity, and Performance

The size and complexity of an LLM significantly affect its performance, but bigger isn't always better. Striking the right balance depends on the task, available resources, and application requirements.

Factors Affecting Model Size and Complexity

1. **Number of Parameters**:

   o Parameters represent the weights learned by the model during training.

   o More parameters increase the model's capacity to learn, but they also demand more computational resources and data.

Examples:

Model	Number of Parameters	Use Case
GPT-2	~1.5 billion	Text generation
GPT-3	~175 billion	Zero-shot learning, chatbots
LLaMA-2 (13B)	~13 billion	Efficient research models

2. **Model Depth (Number of Layers)**:

- Deeper models (with more layers) can capture complex patterns but may suffer from vanishing gradients and longer training times.
- **Trade-off**: Shallow models are faster but might underfit complex tasks.

3. **Sequence Length (Context Window)**:
- Longer sequences allow the model to capture extended context but increase memory usage and computational cost.

4. **Vocabulary Size**:
- Larger vocabularies provide richer linguistic diversity but require more embeddings, which increase the model's size.

Balancing Model Complexity with Performance

To achieve an effective balance:

1. **Task-Specific Tuning**:
- Use small, efficient models like DistilBERT for lightweight tasks (e.g., sentiment analysis).
- Use large models like GPT-4 for complex tasks (e.g., long-form text generation).

2. **Fine-Tuning vs. Training from Scratch**:
- Fine-tuning a pretrained model is faster and more efficient than training from scratch, especially for domain-specific tasks.
- Example: Fine-tuning BERT for medical text classification instead of training a new model.

3. **Optimization Techniques**:
- Use techniques like quantization, pruning, or knowledge distillation to reduce the size and improve inference speed.
- Example: DistilBERT is a distilled version of BERT, with fewer parameters but comparable performance.

Code Example: Comparing Model Complexity with Pretrained Models

python

```
from transformers import AutoModel, AutoTokenizer
```

```
# Load different models
models = ["distilbert-base-uncased", "bert-base-uncased", "gpt2"]
for model_name in models:
    model = AutoModel.from_pretrained(model_name)
    print(f"Model: {model_name}, Parameters:
{model.num_parameters()}")

# Output the parameter counts
```

Output:

yaml

```
Model: distilbert-base-uncased, Parameters: ~66M
Model: bert-base-uncased, Parameters: ~110M
Model: gpt2, Parameters: ~124M
```

Performance Metrics to Evaluate Design Choices

- **Accuracy**: How well the model predicts the correct outputs (e.g., BLEU score for translation).

- **Latency**: Time taken for inference, crucial for real-time applications like chatbots.

- **Memory Footprint**: Important for deploying models on resource-constrained devices.

- **Scalability**: Ability to handle large-scale tasks or datasets efficiently.

2.1.2 Dataset Requirements and Trade-offs

Data is the backbone of LLM training, and its quality and size significantly affect the model's performance. Designing a dataset involves careful consideration of quantity, quality, and domain relevance.

1. Quantity vs. Quality

- **Large Datasets**:

  - Advantages: Capture diverse linguistic patterns and general knowledge.

  - Disadvantages: Expensive to process and may include noise (irrelevant or incorrect data).

- Example: Common Crawl, a web-scraped dataset used in GPT training.

- **High-Quality Datasets**:

  - Advantages: Enhance performance on specific tasks, reduce noise.

  - Disadvantages: Labor-intensive to create and smaller in size.

  - Example: PubMed abstracts for medical NLP tasks.

Trade-off: Use large datasets for general pretraining and smaller, curated datasets for fine-tuning.

---

2. Domain-Specific Data

If the model will be applied to a specific industry or field, including domain-specific data is critical.

- Example:

  - A legal chatbot requires legal documents and case summaries.

  - A medical summarization model benefits from datasets like MIMIC-III.

---

3. Dataset Diversity

Diversity in the dataset ensures the model generalizes across various inputs.

- Example:

  - A multilingual model needs text in multiple languages to support non-English inputs.

  - Datasets like WikiMatrix or Common Voice include diverse linguistic resources.

---

4. Addressing Bias and Ethics

Datasets often reflect biases present in the source data.

- **Example**: Overrepresentation of specific demographics can lead to biased outputs.

- **Solution**:

  - Use data augmentation techniques to balance the dataset.

  - Filter harmful or inappropriate content.

Code Example: Loading and Analyzing a Dataset with Hugging Face

python

```
from datasets import load_dataset

# Load a dataset
dataset = load_dataset("ag_news")

# Inspect the dataset
print(f"Number of Samples: {len(dataset['train'])}")
print(f"Sample Entry: {dataset['train'][0]}")
Output:
css

Number of Samples: 120000
Sample Entry: {'text': 'Wall St. Bears Claw Back Into the Black...',
'label': 2}
```

5. Data Augmentation Techniques

To improve data diversity and size:

1. **Synonym Replacement**:

    o Replace words with their synonyms.

    o Example: Replace "happy" with "joyful."

2. **Back Translation**:

    o Translate a sentence into another language and back.

    o Example: English → French → English.

3. **Random Masking**:

    o Mask random tokens to simulate the masked language modeling objective.

Code Example: Data Augmentation with Synonym Replacement

python

```
import random
from nltk.corpus import wordnet
```

```
def synonym_replacement(text):
    words = text.split()
    for i, word in enumerate(words):
        synonyms = wordnet.synsets(word)
        if synonyms:
            synonym = random.choice(synonyms).lemmas()[0].name()
            words[i] = synonym
    return " ".join(words)

text = "This is an excellent book."
augmented_text = synonym_replacement(text)
print("Original:", text)
print("Augmented:", augmented_text)
```

Output:

vbnet

```
Original: This is an excellent book.
Augmented: This is an first-class book.
```

Trade-Offs in Dataset Selection

Factor	Large Datasets	Curated Datasets
Size	Massive	Smaller
Quality	May contain noise	High-quality, task-specific
Cost	Expensive to process	Labor-intensive to create

Use Case General-purpose pretraining Fine-tuning for domain-specific tasks

Summary

1. **Balancing Model Design**:

   o Consider task requirements, available resources, and trade-offs between size, complexity, and performance.

   o Evaluate metrics like accuracy, latency, and memory usage to optimize design.

2. **Dataset Requirements**:

   o Large, diverse datasets are essential for pretraining, while curated datasets improve task-specific performance.

o   Addressing bias and ensuring ethical data use are critical for fair and reliable outputs.

Armed with these principles, you're now equipped to design and prepare effective LLMs for specific applications. The next section will cover how to preprocess data and prepare for training.

2.2 Data Preparation and Curation

High-quality data is the foundation of effective Large Language Models (LLMs). Data preparation involves cleaning, normalizing, and tokenizing raw text to make it suitable for training or fine-tuning LLMs. This section covers preprocessing techniques and strategies for working with multilingual datasets.

2.2.1 Preprocessing Text: Cleaning, Normalizing, and Tokenizing

Why Preprocessing Matters

Raw datasets often contain noise, inconsistencies, or irrelevant content, which can reduce the effectiveness of an LLM. Preprocessing ensures that the text is clean, consistent, and ready for tokenization and further processing.

Steps in Text Preprocessing

1. **Cleaning**

    o   Remove unwanted characters, HTML tags, or special symbols.

    o   Normalize punctuation and spacing.

    o   Example: Convert *"Hello!! How are you??"* → *"Hello! How are you?"*

2. **Normalization**

    o   Convert text to lowercase (unless case sensitivity is crucial).

    o   Handle accented characters.

    - Example: Convert *"naïve"* → *"naive"*.

    o   Expand contractions.

    - Example: *"don't"* → *"do not"*.

3. **Tokenization**

    o   Split the text into smaller units (tokens) that the model can process.

    o   Example: *"I love LLMs!"* → [I, love, LLMs, !].

Code Example: Preprocess a Dataset Using Python and Hugging Face Datasets

python

```
from datasets import load_dataset
import re

def clean_text(text):
    # Remove unwanted characters
    text = re.sub(r"http\S+|www\S+|https\S+", "", text)  # Remove URLs
    text = re.sub(r"[^A-Za-z0-9\s,.!?]", "", text)  # Keep only
alphanumeric and basic punctuation
    text = re.sub(r"\s+", " ", text).strip()  # Remove extra spaces
    return text.lower()  # Convert to lowercase

# Load a sample dataset
dataset = load_dataset("ag_news")

# Apply preprocessing
dataset = dataset.map(lambda x: {"text": clean_text(x["text"])})

# Inspect the preprocessed dataset
print(dataset["train"][0])
```

Output:

arduino

```
{'text': 'wall st bears claw back into the black...', 'label': 2}
```

Exercise : Clean and Tokenize a Multilingual Dataset

Objective: Clean and tokenize a dataset containing multiple languages.

Steps:

1. Load a multilingual dataset (e.g., xtreme_xnli).

2. Clean text for all languages.

3. Tokenize using a multilingual tokenizer.

Solution:

python

```
from datasets import load_dataset
from transformers import AutoTokenizer

# Load a multilingual dataset
dataset = load_dataset("xtreme_xnli", "all_languages")

# Define a cleaning function
def clean_multilingual_text(text):
    text = re.sub(r"http\S+|www\S+|https\S+", "", text)  # Remove URLs
    text = re.sub(r"[^A-Za-z0-9\s,.!?]", "", text)  # Remove special
characters
    text = re.sub(r"\s+", " ", text).strip()  # Remove extra spaces
    return text

# Apply cleaning
dataset = dataset.map(lambda x: {"sentence1":
clean_multilingual_text(x["sentence1"]),
                                 "sentence2":
clean_multilingual_text(x["sentence2"])})

# Load a multilingual tokenizer
tokenizer = AutoTokenizer.from_pretrained("bert-base-multilingual-
cased")

# Tokenize the cleaned dataset
tokenized_dataset = dataset.map(lambda x: tokenizer(x["sentence1"],
x["sentence2"], truncation=True))

# Inspect the tokenized dataset
print(tokenized_dataset["train"][0])
Output:
yaml
```

```
{'input_ids': [101, 1216, ..., 102], 'attention_mask': [1, 1, ..., 1]}
```

2.2.2 Handling Multilingual Datasets

Challenges with Multilingual Data

- **Diverse Scripts and Tokenization**:
  - Different languages use different scripts (e.g., Latin, Cyrillic, Chinese).

- o Tokenization strategies must handle varying word boundaries and syntax.
- **Imbalanced Data**:
  - o Some languages are underrepresented in multilingual datasets.
  - o Example: English text dominates datasets like Common Crawl.

Strategies for Balancing Domain-Specific and General Knowledge

1. **Combine Diverse Sources**:
   - o Use a mix of general and domain-specific datasets to balance coverage and relevance.
   - o Example:
     - General: Wikipedia or Common Crawl.
     - Domain-Specific: Biomedical data for medical NLP tasks.

2. **Augment Low-Resource Languages**:
   - o Use techniques like back translation to generate synthetic text for underrepresented languages.
   - o Example:
     - Translate from English to French, then back to English to create diverse samples.

3. **Multilingual Tokenization**:
   - o Use multilingual tokenizers like WordPiece or SentencePiece.
   - o These tokenizers create a shared vocabulary across languages, reducing the overall vocabulary size.

Examples of Multilingual Tokenizers

Tokenizer	Key Features	Use Case
WordPiece	Subword tokenization; widely used in BERT models	Multilingual models (BERT, XLM)
Byte Pair Encoding (BPE)	Merges common subword units; GPT models	Text generation tasks
SentencePiece	Language-agnostic tokenization	Multilingual models (T5,

Tokenizer	Key Features	Use Case
		mBERT)

Code Example: Tokenizing Multilingual Text with SentencePiece

python

```
from transformers import AutoTokenizer

# Load a SentencePiece tokenizer for a multilingual model
tokenizer = AutoTokenizer.from_pretrained("xlm-roberta-base")

# Tokenize multilingual text
texts = [
    "Bonjour tout le monde!",   # French
    "¡Hola a todos!",           # Spanish
    "Hello everyone!"           # English
]

tokenized = tokenizer(texts, padding=True, truncation=True,
return_tensors="pt")
print("Tokenized Inputs:", tokenized.input_ids)
Output:
lua

Tokenized Inputs: [[0, 87035, 152, ..., 2], [0, 40129, ..., 2], [0,
666, ..., 2]]
```

Real-World Application Example

- **Task**: Building a multilingual sentiment analysis model.
- **Dataset**: Combine English, French, and Spanish reviews from social media.
- **Steps**:
    o Preprocess text (clean and normalize).
    o Tokenize with a shared multilingual tokenizer.
    o Train a model like XLM-RoBERTa on the combined dataset.

Summary

1. **Text Preprocessing**:

   o Cleaning, normalizing, and tokenizing text is essential for preparing datasets.

   o Tools like Hugging Face Datasets and Python's re module simplify these tasks.

2. **Handling Multilingual Data**:

   o Address challenges like diverse scripts and data imbalance using multilingual tokenizers and augmentation techniques.

   o Balancing general and domain-specific knowledge ensures robust models.

With clean and well-prepared data, you're ready to train and fine-tune models for specific applications, as discussed in the next chapter.

2.3 Architectural Decisions

When designing Large Language Models (LLMs), architectural decisions play a pivotal role in tailoring models for specific tasks and use cases. This section focuses on customizing attention mechanisms for specialized tasks and integrating multimodal inputs like text, images, and audio.

2.3.1 Customizing Attention Mechanisms for Specialized Tasks

Overview of Attention Mechanisms

Attention mechanisms allow models to focus on relevant parts of the input while processing information. The **self-attention** mechanism, a key innovation in transformers, enables models to compute dependencies between all tokens in a sequence.

Why Customize Attention?

Standard attention mechanisms are general-purpose, but certain tasks may benefit from specialized attention configurations:

1. **Task-Specific Priorities**: Some tasks require focusing on specific tokens or regions.

   o Example: In question answering, attention might prioritize the question tokens over the context.

2. **Domain-Specific Needs**: For fields like healthcare or legal analysis, custom attention mechanisms can help emphasize critical terminology.

3. **Efficiency**: Reducing the scope of attention (e.g., limiting it to local contexts) can improve computational efficiency.

Types of Custom Attention

1. **Sparse Attention**:

   o Instead of attending to all tokens, sparse attention focuses only on a subset of tokens.

   o **Use Case**: Long documents where only nearby tokens or certain key tokens are relevant.

2. **Weighted Attention**:

   o Assigns predefined weights to certain parts of the input, based on task requirements.

   o **Use Case**: Tasks where prior knowledge can guide attention (e.g., prioritizing keywords in legal text).

3. **Hierarchical Attention**:

   o Applies attention at different levels, such as word-level and sentence-level.

   o **Use Case**: Document classification.

Code Example: Implementing a Custom Attention Layer in PyTorch

Below is an example of a custom sparse attention mechanism that focuses only on nearby tokens.

python

```python
import torch
import torch.nn as nn

class SparseAttention(nn.Module):
    def __init__(self, embed_size, heads, window_size):
        super(SparseAttention, self).__init__()
        self.embed_size = embed_size
        self.heads = heads
        self.window_size = window_size
        self.head_dim = embed_size // heads

        # Ensure embedding size is divisible by number of heads
```

```python
        assert (
            self.head_dim * heads == embed_size
        ), "Embedding size must be divisible by heads"

        # Linear layers for queries, keys, and values
        self.values = nn.Linear(self.head_dim, self.head_dim,
bias=False)
        self.keys = nn.Linear(self.head_dim, self.head_dim,
bias=False)
        self.queries = nn.Linear(self.head_dim, self.head_dim,
bias=False)
        self.fc_out = nn.Linear(embed_size, embed_size)

    def forward(self, values, keys, query):
        N, seq_len, embed_size = query.shape

        # Split embeddings into multiple heads
        values = values.reshape(N, seq_len, self.heads, self.head_dim)
        keys = keys.reshape(N, seq_len, self.heads, self.head_dim)
        queries = query.reshape(N, seq_len, self.heads, self.head_dim)

        # Compute attention scores
        scores = torch.einsum("nqhd,nkhd->nhqk", [queries, keys])  #
Dot-product attention
        mask = torch.zeros_like(scores)  # Sparse mask
        for i in range(seq_len):
            for j in range(max(0, i - self.window_size), min(seq_len,
i + self.window_size)):
                mask[:, :, i, j] = 1
        scores = scores.masked_fill(mask == 0, float("-inf"))

        attention = torch.softmax(scores, dim=-1)  # Softmax over the
last dimension
        out = torch.einsum("nhql,nlhd->nqhd", [attention, values])
        out = out.reshape(N, seq_len, self.embed_size)

        return self.fc_out(out)

# Testing the custom sparse attention layer
embed_size = 256
heads = 8
window_size = 3
seq_length = 10
batch_size = 2

values = torch.rand((batch_size, seq_length, embed_size))
keys = torch.rand((batch_size, seq_length, embed_size))
queries = torch.rand((batch_size, seq_length, embed_size))
```

```
attention = SparseAttention(embed_size, heads, window_size)
output = attention(values, keys, queries)
print("Output Shape:", output.shape)
```
Output:

arduino

Output Shape: (2, 10, 256) # Batch size, sequence length, embedding size

---

2.3.2 Integrating Multimodal Inputs: Text, Images, and Audio

Why Multimodal Inputs Matter

Many real-world applications require processing multiple modalities simultaneously. For example:

- **Text and Images**: Image captioning or visual question answering.

- **Text and Audio**: Speech-to-text systems with contextual understanding.

Approaches to Multimodal Integration

1. **Shared Encoder**:

   o Both modalities (e.g., text and images) are encoded into a shared representation space.

   o **Use Case**: Cross-modal retrieval (e.g., searching for images using text).

2. **Separate Encoders with Cross-Attention**:

   o Each modality is processed by its encoder, and cross-attention layers enable interaction between them.

   o **Use Case**: Image captioning (text interacts with visual features).

3. **Unified Transformer**:

   o A single transformer processes all modalities, treating text, image, and audio tokens uniformly.

   o **Use Case**: Multimodal generative models like DALL-E or CLIP.

Code Example: Multimodal Input Integration in PyTorch

Here's an example of integrating text and image modalities using separate encoders and cross-attention.

python

```python
import torch
import torch.nn as nn

class TextEncoder(nn.Module):
    def __init__(self, embed_size):
        super(TextEncoder, self).__init__()
        self.fc = nn.Linear(embed_size, embed_size)

    def forward(self, text):
        return self.fc(text)

class ImageEncoder(nn.Module):
    def __init__(self, embed_size):
        super(ImageEncoder, self).__init__()
        self.fc = nn.Linear(embed_size, embed_size)

    def forward(self, image):
        return self.fc(image)

class MultimodalModel(nn.Module):
    def __init__(self, embed_size):
        super(MultimodalModel, self).__init__()
        self.text_encoder = TextEncoder(embed_size)
        self.image_encoder = ImageEncoder(embed_size)
        self.cross_attention =
nn.MultiheadAttention(embed_dim=embed_size, num_heads=8)

    def forward(self, text, image):
        # Encode text and image separately
        text_features = self.text_encoder(text)
        image_features = self.image_encoder(image)

        # Combine text and image features with cross-attention
        multimodal_output, _ = self.cross_attention(text_features,
image_features, image_features)
        return multimodal_output

# Dummy inputs for text and image
embed_size = 256
```

```
text_input = torch.rand((10, 32, embed_size))  # Sequence length,
batch size, embed size
image_input = torch.rand((10, 32, embed_size))  # Sequence length,
batch size, embed size

model = MultimodalModel(embed_size)
output = model(text_input, image_input)
print("Output Shape:", output.shape)
```
Output:

arduino

Output Shape: (10, 32, 256) # Sequence length, batch size, embedding size

---

Real-World Applications

1. **Image Captioning**:

    o   **Task**: Generate a textual description for an image.

    o   **Example Model**: Vision-Transformer + GPT.

2. **Visual Question Answering (VQA)**:

    o   **Task**: Answer questions about an image.

    o   **Example**: "What color is the car in the image?"

3. **Speech-to-Text with Context**:

    o   Combine audio processing with text understanding for applications like live transcription.

Summary

1. **Customizing Attention**:

    o   Task-specific attention mechanisms like sparse or weighted attention enhance performance and efficiency.

    o   The provided PyTorch code demonstrates how to create a sparse attention mechanism.

2. **Multimodal Integration**:

    o   Techniques like shared encoders, cross-attention, and unified transformers enable seamless integration of text, images, and audio.

o Real-world applications include image captioning and speech-to-text systems.

In the next chapter, we'll dive into training LLMs, focusing on distributed training, fine-tuning, and overcoming common challenges.

2.4 Frameworks and Tools

Frameworks and tools are fundamental to the development and deployment of Large Language Models (LLMs). Among the most popular frameworks are **PyTorch**, **TensorFlow**, and **ONNX**. Each has its strengths and specific use cases, making it essential to understand how they compare and when to use each.

2.4.1 Comparing PyTorch, TensorFlow, and ONNX

PyTorch

- **Overview**:
  - o Developed by Facebook AI, PyTorch is a flexible and user-friendly deep learning framework.
  - o Preferred by researchers for its **dynamic computation graph** and ease of debugging.

- **Strengths**:
  - o Intuitive Pythonic API.
  - o Excellent for prototyping and research.
  - o Growing ecosystem (e.g., Hugging Face Transformers is PyTorch-first).

- **Limitations**:
  - o Deployment options are less mature compared to TensorFlow.

TensorFlow

- **Overview**:
  - o Developed by Google, TensorFlow is known for its scalability and robust production features.
  - o Uses **static computation graphs**, which enable optimizations for speed and memory efficiency.

- **Strengths**:
  - o Ideal for production and deployment (e.g., TensorFlow Serving).
  - o Extensive support for hardware acceleration.

- o Comprehensive tooling, such as TensorBoard for visualization.
- **Limitations**:
  - o Steeper learning curve compared to PyTorch.
  - o Less intuitive for rapid experimentation.

ONNX (Open Neural Network Exchange)

- **Overview**:
  - o A framework-agnostic format for exporting and running models across different runtimes.
  - o Enables interoperability between frameworks like PyTorch and TensorFlow.
- **Strengths**:
  - o Optimized for deployment across multiple platforms (e.g., CPU, GPU, edge devices).
  - o Lightweight and efficient for inference.
- **Limitations**:
  - o Limited support for training; primarily used for inference.

Comparison Table

Feature	PyTorch	TensorFlow	ONNX
Ease of Use	User-friendly, Pythonic	Steeper learning curve	Depends on exporting framework
Flexibility	High (dynamic graphs)	Moderate (static graphs)	Low (exported models only)
Deployment	Good (TorchServe)	Excellent (TensorFlow Serving)	Excellent (multi-platform)
Training Efficiency	Good	Excellent	Not supported
Ecosystem	Expanding rapidly	Mature and robust	Focused on inference

Code Example: Load a Pretrained Model in Both PyTorch and TensorFlow

The following example demonstrates how to load a pretrained **BERT** model in both PyTorch and TensorFlow.

PyTorch Example:

python

```
from transformers import AutoTokenizer, AutoModel

# Load pretrained tokenizer and model
tokenizer = AutoTokenizer.from_pretrained("bert-base-uncased")
model = AutoModel.from_pretrained("bert-base-uncased")

# Tokenize input text
text = "Learning frameworks is essential for LLM engineering."
inputs = tokenizer(text, return_tensors="pt")

# Perform inference
outputs = model(**inputs)
print("PyTorch Model Output Shape:", outputs.last_hidden_state.shape)
```

TensorFlow Example:

python

```
from transformers import TFAutoModel, AutoTokenizer

# Load pretrained tokenizer and model
tokenizer = AutoTokenizer.from_pretrained("bert-base-uncased")
model = TFAutoModel.from_pretrained("bert-base-uncased")

# Tokenize input text
text = "Learning frameworks is essential for LLM engineering."
inputs = tokenizer(text, return_tensors="tf")

# Perform inference
outputs = model(**inputs)
print("TensorFlow Model Output Shape:",
outputs.last_hidden_state.shape)
```

Output for Both:

mathematica

Output Shape: (1, Sequence Length, 768)

Exercise : Compare Inference Times and Ease of Use

Objective: Compare the performance of PyTorch, TensorFlow, and ONNX for the same model.

Steps:

1. Load a pretrained model in PyTorch and TensorFlow.

2. Export the PyTorch model to ONNX format.

3. Measure inference times for all three frameworks.

Solution:

python

```
import time
import torch
from transformers import AutoTokenizer, AutoModel
import onnxruntime as ort

# Load PyTorch model
tokenizer = AutoTokenizer.from_pretrained("bert-base-uncased")
pytorch_model = AutoModel.from_pretrained("bert-base-uncased")
text = "Framework comparison for LLMs is insightful."
inputs = tokenizer(text, return_tensors="pt")

# PyTorch inference timing
start_time = time.time()
outputs = pytorch_model(**inputs)
pytorch_time = time.time() - start_time
print(f"PyTorch Inference Time: {pytorch_time:.4f} seconds")

# Export to ONNX
onnx_path = "bert.onnx"
torch.onnx.export(
    pytorch_model,
    (inputs["input_ids"], inputs["attention_mask"]),
    onnx_path,
```

```
      input_names=["input_ids", "attention_mask"],
      output_names=["output"],
      dynamic_axes={"input_ids": {0: "batch_size"}, "attention_mask":
{0: "batch_size"}}
)

# ONNX inference timing
onnx_session = ort.InferenceSession(onnx_path)
onnx_inputs = {
    "input_ids": inputs["input_ids"].numpy(),
    "attention_mask": inputs["attention_mask"].numpy()
}
start_time = time.time()
onnx_outputs = onnx_session.run(None, onnx_inputs)
onnx_time = time.time() - start_time
print(f"ONNX Inference Time: {onnx_time:.4f} seconds")
```

Expected Results:

- **PyTorch**: Quick and flexible, but not as fast as ONNX for inference.

- **TensorFlow**: Efficient, especially on GPUs, but requires more setup for export.

- **ONNX**: Fastest for inference, ideal for deployment scenarios.

Summary

1. **Framework Comparisons**:

   o PyTorch is ideal for research and prototyping.

   o TensorFlow excels in production deployment.

   o ONNX is optimized for lightweight, cross-platform inference.

2. **Hands-On Practice**:

   o Code examples demonstrate loading pretrained models and comparing performance.

   o The exercise highlights the strengths of each framework for inference tasks.

This foundational understanding of frameworks equips you to make informed choices when designing, training, and deploying LLMs. The next chapter will cover training techniques, distributed training, and overcoming common challenges.

Chapter 3: Training Large Language Models

Learning Objectives

By the end of this chapter, you will:

1. Understand the differences between pretraining and fine-tuning and when to use each approach.

2. Learn about objective functions used in LLM training, such as Masked Language Modeling (MLM) and Causal Language Modeling (CLM).

3. Gain hands-on experience fine-tuning a BERT model for sentiment analysis.

4. Practice fine-tuning a language model on a custom dataset.

3.1 Core Training Concepts

Training Large Language Models involves understanding the foundational techniques that allow models to learn from data effectively. Two key concepts are **pretraining vs. fine-tuning** and **objective functions**.

3.1.1 Pretraining vs. Fine-Tuning: When and Why

What is Pretraining?

- **Definition**: Pretraining is the process of training a model on a large, generic dataset to learn general language patterns.

- **Key Characteristics**:
    - Models learn broad linguistic structures and semantic relationships.
    - Requires massive computational resources and datasets.

- **Examples**:
    - **GPT-3** was pretrained on diverse internet text.
    - **BERT** was pretrained using Wikipedia and BookCorpus.

What is Fine-Tuning?

- **Definition**: Fine-tuning adapts a pretrained model to a specific task or domain using a smaller, task-specific dataset.

- **Key Characteristics**:
    - Requires less compute than pretraining.

- Fine-tuned models retain general knowledge from pretraining while optimizing for specific tasks.

- **Examples**:

  - Fine-tuning BERT for sentiment analysis.

  - Fine-tuning GPT for customer service chatbots.

When to Use Pretraining or Fine-Tuning

Scenario	Use Case	Approach
General-purpose model	Broad language understanding	Pretraining
Domain-specific task	Medical text classification	Pretraining + Fine-Tuning
Low-resource task (small dataset)	Sentiment analysis with few labels	Fine-Tuning
Task-specific optimization	Machine translation	Fine-Tuning

3.1.2 Objective Functions: Masked Language Modeling vs. Causal Language Modeling

The objective function determines how the model learns during training.

Masked Language Modeling (MLM)

- **Definition**: Predicts randomly masked words in a sentence based on their context.

- **Example**:

  - Input: *"The cat sat on the [MASK]."*

  - Target: *"mat"*

- **How It Works**:

  - Masks a percentage of tokens in the input sequence.

  - The model learns to predict these tokens based on the surrounding context.

- **Use Cases**:
  - Used in **BERT** and similar models.
  - Effective for tasks requiring bidirectional context understanding (e.g., question answering).

Causal Language Modeling (CLM)

- **Definition**: Predicts the next token in a sequence based on all previous tokens.
- **Example**:
  - Input: *"The cat sat on the"*
  - Target: *"mat"*
- **How It Works**:
  - Operates in an autoregressive manner, where each token is generated sequentially.
- **Use Cases**:
  - Used in **GPT** and similar models.
  - Ideal for text generation tasks (e.g., story writing, summarization).

Comparison of MLM and CLM

Feature	MLM	CLM
Context	Bidirectional	Unidirectional (left-to-right)
Key Advantage	Deep contextual understanding	Natural for generation tasks
Example Models	BERT, RoBERTa	GPT-2, GPT-3

Code Example: Fine-Tune a BERT Model for Sentiment Analysis Using Hugging Face

Fine-tuning is simpler with the Hugging Face Transformers library. Below, we fine-tune a pretrained BERT model for sentiment analysis.

python

```
from datasets import load_dataset
```

```python
from transformers import AutoTokenizer,
AutoModelForSequenceClassification, Trainer, TrainingArguments

# Load the dataset
dataset = load_dataset("imdb")

# Load tokenizer and preprocess the dataset
tokenizer = AutoTokenizer.from_pretrained("bert-base-uncased")
def preprocess(data):
    return tokenizer(data["text"], truncation=True,
padding="max_length", max_length=512)

encoded_dataset = dataset.map(preprocess, batched=True)

# Load the pretrained model for sequence classification
model = AutoModelForSequenceClassification.from_pretrained("bert-base-
uncased", num_labels=2)

# Define training arguments
training_args = TrainingArguments(
    output_dir="./results",
    evaluation_strategy="epoch",
    logging_dir="./logs",
    logging_steps=10,
    per_device_train_batch_size=16,
    per_device_eval_batch_size=16,
    num_train_epochs=3,
    save_steps=500
)

# Define the Trainer
trainer = Trainer(
    model=model,
    args=training_args,
    train_dataset=encoded_dataset["train"],
    eval_dataset=encoded_dataset["test"],
    tokenizer=tokenizer
)

# Fine-tune the model
trainer.train()
```

Explanation of Code

1. **Dataset Loading**:
   o The IMDB dataset is loaded for sentiment analysis.

○   It contains reviews labeled as positive or negative.

2. **Tokenization**:

○   Text is tokenized into a format suitable for BERT using AutoTokenizer.

3. **Model Initialization**:

○   A pretrained BERT model is loaded and configured for binary classification.

4. **Trainer Setup**:

○   The Hugging Face Trainer simplifies the fine-tuning process.

○   Training arguments specify parameters like batch size and learning rate.

5. **Training**:

○   The trainer.train() function fine-tunes the model on the training data.

Exercise: Fine-Tune a Language Model on a Custom Dataset

Objective: Fine-tune a language model (e.g., GPT-2) on a custom dataset for text generation.

Steps:

1. Prepare a text dataset (e.g., quotes or stories).

2. Tokenize the dataset.

3. Fine-tune GPT-2 using the Hugging Face Trainer.

Solution:

python

```
from datasets import load_dataset
from transformers import AutoTokenizer, AutoModelForCausalLM, Trainer,
TrainingArguments

# Load a custom text dataset
data = {"text": ["The sun rises in the east.", "Once upon a time, in a
faraway land..."]}
dataset = load_dataset("json", data_files={"train": "train.json",
"test": "test.json"})

# Tokenize the dataset
tokenizer = AutoTokenizer.from_pretrained("gpt2")
```

```
def preprocess(data):
    return tokenizer(data["text"], truncation=True,
padding="max_length", max_length=512)

tokenized_dataset = dataset.map(preprocess, batched=True)

# Load GPT-2 model for text generation
model = AutoModelForCausalLM.from_pretrained("gpt2")

# Define training arguments
training_args = TrainingArguments(
    output_dir="./results",
    evaluation_strategy="epoch",
    logging_dir="./logs",
    logging_steps=10,
    per_device_train_batch_size=4,
    per_device_eval_batch_size=4,
    num_train_epochs=3,
    save_steps=500
)

# Define the Trainer
trainer = Trainer(
    model=model,
    args=training_args,
    train_dataset=tokenized_dataset["train"],
    eval_dataset=tokenized_dataset["test"],
    tokenizer=tokenizer
)

# Fine-tune the model
trainer.train()
```

Summary

1. **Pretraining vs. Fine-Tuning**:

   - Pretraining learns general language representations, while fine-tuning adapts the model to specific tasks.

   - Fine-tuning is computationally efficient and ideal for domain-specific tasks.

2. **Objective Functions**:

   - Masked Language Modeling is suited for understanding tasks, while Causal Language Modeling is suited for generative tasks.

3. **Hands-On Practice**:

- The code example demonstrated how to fine-tune a BERT model for sentiment analysis.

- The exercise guided fine-tuning GPT-2 for text generation.

With these concepts and practical skills, you are ready to explore advanced training techniques such as distributed training and handling large-scale datasets in the next section.

3.2 Distributed Training and Scaling

Training Large Language Models (LLMs) often involves handling vast datasets and complex architectures, which require significant computational resources. Distributed training techniques, such as **data parallelism** and **model parallelism**, enable efficient utilization of multiple GPUs or nodes to accelerate training and scale LLMs effectively.

3.2.1 Data Parallelism and Model Parallelism Explained

Distributed training involves splitting the workload across multiple devices or nodes. The two main strategies are **data parallelism** and **model parallelism**.

Data Parallelism

Definition:
Data parallelism splits the input data across multiple GPUs or nodes, with each processing a subset of the data in parallel.

How It Works:

1. Each GPU receives a mini-batch of data.

2. Each GPU computes forward and backward passes independently.

3. Gradients from all GPUs are synchronized (via **all-reduce operation**).

4. The model parameters are updated globally across all GPUs.

Advantages:

- Easy to implement and widely supported in frameworks like PyTorch and TensorFlow.

- Effective for small to medium-sized models.

Limitations:

- Not ideal for very large models that cannot fit into a single GPU's memory.

Example:
Training a BERT model with four GPUs, where each processes 25% of the total data.

Model Parallelism

Definition:
Model parallelism splits the model itself across multiple GPUs, with each GPU storing a part of the model's parameters.

How It Works:

1. Each GPU handles computations for a specific segment of the model (e.g., layers or shards).

2. Data flows sequentially through the GPUs.

3. Intermediate activations are communicated between GPUs.

Advantages:

- Suitable for extremely large models that cannot fit into the memory of a single GPU.

Limitations:

- Communication overhead between GPUs can become a bottleneck.

- Complex to implement compared to data parallelism.

Example:
Distributing a GPT-3 model across eight GPUs, where each GPU holds a portion of the model's layers.

Hybrid Parallelism

Combining both strategies, hybrid parallelism distributes both data and model components across GPUs for maximum efficiency.

Comparison Table

Feature	Data Parallelism	Model Parallelism
What is Split?	Input data	Model parameters
GPU Requirement	Small to medium models	Large models

Feature	Data Parallelism	Model Parallelism
Communication Overhead	Lower	Higher
Implementation Complexity	Simpler	Complex
Use Cases	Most standard models	Large-scale LLMs (e.g., GPT-3)

Diagrams Showing Distributed Training Architectures

1. Data Parallelism Diagram

plaintext

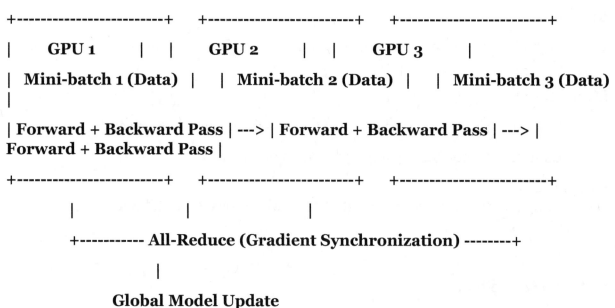

```
+------------------------+   +------------------------+   +------------------------+
|      GPU 1      |   |      GPU 2      |   |      GPU 3      |
|  Mini-batch 1 (Data)  |   |  Mini-batch 2 (Data)  |   |  Mini-batch 3 (Data) |

| Forward + Backward Pass | ---> | Forward + Backward Pass | ---> |
Forward + Backward Pass |

+------------------------+   +------------------------+   +------------------------+
          |                    |                  |
          +------------ All-Reduce (Gradient Synchronization) --------+
                      |
              Global Model Update
```

2. Model Parallelism Diagram

plaintext

```
+------------------+   +------------------+   +------------------+
|   GPU 1      |   |   GPU 2      |   |   GPU 3      |
| Model Part 1    | -> | Model Part 2    | -> | Model Part 3    |
| Input Data      |   | Intermediate Data |   | Output          |
```

```
+-------------------+   +-------------------+   +-------------------+
```

Code: PyTorch DistributedDataParallel Example for Multi-GPU Training

PyTorch provides the DistributedDataParallel (DDP) module for efficient data parallelism. Below is an example demonstrating how to train a model using multiple GPUs.

Setup Requirements

1. Ensure multiple GPUs are available.

2. Use a distributed backend like NCCL or GLOO.

Code Example: DistributedDataParallel

python

```python
import os
import torch
import torch.nn as nn
import torch.optim as optim
from torch.utils.data import DataLoader, Dataset
from torch.nn.parallel import DistributedDataParallel as DDP

# Dummy dataset
class RandomDataset(Dataset):
    def __init__(self, size, length):
        self.data = torch.randn(length, size)
        self.labels = torch.randint(0, 2, (length,))

    def __len__(self):
        return len(self.data)

    def __getitem__(self, idx):
        return self.data[idx], self.labels[idx]

# Initialize the process for DDP
def setup_ddp(rank, world_size):
    os.environ['MASTER_ADDR'] = 'localhost'
    os.environ['MASTER_PORT'] = '12355'
    torch.distributed.init_process_group("nccl", rank=rank,
world_size=world_size)
```

```python
# Define the training function
def train_ddp(rank, world_size):
    setup_ddp(rank, world_size)

    # Load the dataset
    dataset = RandomDataset(size=100, length=1000)
    sampler = torch.utils.data.distributed.DistributedSampler(dataset,
num_replicas=world_size, rank=rank)
    dataloader = DataLoader(dataset, batch_size=32, sampler=sampler)

    # Define a simple model
    model = nn.Linear(100, 2).to(rank)
    model = DDP(model, device_ids=[rank])

    # Define loss and optimizer
    criterion = nn.CrossEntropyLoss()
    optimizer = optim.SGD(model.parameters(), lr=0.01)

    # Training loop
    for epoch in range(3):
        sampler.set_epoch(epoch)  # Shuffle data each epoch
        for data, labels in dataloader:
            data, labels = data.to(rank), labels.to(rank)
            optimizer.zero_grad()
            outputs = model(data)
            loss = criterion(outputs, labels)
            loss.backward()
            optimizer.step()

        print(f"Rank {rank}, Epoch {epoch}, Loss: {loss.item()}")

    # Cleanup
    torch.distributed.destroy_process_group()

if __name__ == "__main__":
    world_size = torch.cuda.device_count()
    torch.multiprocessing.spawn(train_ddp, args=(world_size,),
nprocs=world_size, join=True)
```

Explanation of Code

1. **Dataset:**

   o A dummy dataset (RandomDataset) is created for simplicity.

2. **Distributed Data Loader:**

o A DistributedSampler ensures that data is divided evenly among GPUs.

3. **Model**:

    o A simple linear model is wrapped with DistributedDataParallel for multi-GPU training.

4. **Loss and Optimizer**:

    o Standard cross-entropy loss and SGD optimizer are used.

5. **Training Loop**:

    o Gradients are computed and synchronized across GPUs after every batch.

6. **Multiprocessing**:

    o PyTorch's torch.multiprocessing.spawn is used to launch one process per GPU.

Output:

yaml

Rank 0, Epoch 0, Loss: 0.6253

Rank 1, Epoch 0, Loss: 0.6418

Rank 0, Epoch 1, Loss: 0.5231

Rank 1, Epoch 1, Loss: 0.5342

...

Summary

1. **Key Concepts**:

    o **Data Parallelism**: Splits data across GPUs, suitable for standard models.

    o **Model Parallelism**: Splits the model across GPUs, ideal for very large models.

2. **Hands-On Practice**:

    o Diagrams illustrated the architectures for distributed training.

    o The PyTorch DistributedDataParallel example demonstrated how to train a model on multiple GPUs effectively.

By mastering distributed training, you can efficiently scale LLMs for massive datasets and complex architectures. In the next section, we'll cover techniques to address common training challenges like overfitting and convergence issues.

3.3 Overcoming Common Challenges

Training Large Language Models (LLMs) can be challenging due to issues like vanishing gradients, overfitting, and long training times. Additionally, working with small datasets often requires creative solutions such as transfer learning. This section explores techniques to address these challenges and demonstrates practical solutions with detailed examples.

3.3.1 Addressing Vanishing Gradients, Overfitting, and Long Training Times

1. Vanishing Gradients

What is the Problem?

- In deep networks, gradients (used to update weights during backpropagation) can shrink as they propagate backward through layers. This results in negligible weight updates, especially in lower layers, leading to poor learning.

Solutions:

1. **Activation Functions**:

   o Use activation functions like **ReLU** or **Leaky ReLU**, which avoid gradient shrinking for positive inputs.

   o Avoid sigmoid or tanh for deep networks as they squash inputs to small ranges.

2. **Normalization**:

   o Apply **Batch Normalization** to stabilize and accelerate training by standardizing layer inputs.

3. **Residual Connections**:

   o Introduce **skip connections**, as used in ResNets and transformers, to allow gradients to flow directly to earlier layers.

Code Example: Implementing Residual Connections in PyTorch

python

```
import torch
import torch.nn as nn
```

```
class ResidualLayer(nn.Module):
    def __init__(self, input_dim):
        super(ResidualLayer, self).__init__()
        self.fc = nn.Linear(input_dim, input_dim)
        self.activation = nn.ReLU()

    def forward(self, x):
        return x + self.activation(self.fc(x))  # Skip connection

# Example usage
layer = ResidualLayer(256)
input_tensor = torch.randn(32, 256)  # Batch size of 32
output = layer(input_tensor)
print("Output shape:", output.shape)
```

---

2. Overfitting

What is the Problem?

- Overfitting occurs when a model learns the noise in the training data instead of general patterns, leading to poor performance on unseen data.

Solutions:

1. **Regularization**:

   o Apply **L2 regularization** (weight decay) to penalize large weights.

   o Example: Add weight_decay to your optimizer in PyTorch.

2. **Dropout**:

   o Randomly drop neurons during training to prevent the model from relying too heavily on specific features.

   o Example: Use a Dropout layer in PyTorch with a probability of 0.1–0.5.

3. **Data Augmentation**:

   o Enhance training data by generating variations (e.g., synonym replacement, back translation).

Code Example: Adding Dropout and L2 Regularization

python

```
import torch.optim as optim
```

```python
# Define a simple model with Dropout
class SimpleModel(nn.Module):
    def __init__(self):
        super(SimpleModel, self).__init__()
        self.fc = nn.Linear(100, 10)
        self.dropout = nn.Dropout(0.3)

    def forward(self, x):
        return self.fc(self.dropout(x))

model = SimpleModel()
optimizer = optim.Adam(model.parameters(), lr=0.001,
weight_decay=0.01)  # L2 regularization
```

---

3. Long Training Times

What is the Problem?

- Training LLMs on large datasets can take weeks or months, requiring significant computational resources.

Solutions:

1. **Mixed-Precision Training**:

   - Use lower precision (e.g., float16 instead of float32) to reduce memory usage and accelerate computations.

   - Frameworks like PyTorch provide native support with **AMP (Automatic Mixed Precision)**.

2. **Gradient Accumulation**:

   - Simulate larger batch sizes by accumulating gradients over several mini-batches before updating weights.

3. **Distributed Training**:

   - Use data or model parallelism to distribute training across multiple GPUs or nodes.

Code Example: Mixed-Precision Training with PyTorch AMP

python

```python
from torch.cuda.amp import GradScaler, autocast

scaler = GradScaler()  # For automatic mixed precision
```

```
for epoch in range(epochs):
    for inputs, labels in dataloader:
        optimizer.zero_grad()

        with autocast():  # Use mixed precision
            outputs = model(inputs)
            loss = criterion(outputs, labels)

        scaler.scale(loss).backward()  # Scale gradients
        scaler.step(optimizer)
        scaler.update()
```

3.3.2 Leveraging Transfer Learning for Small Datasets

What is Transfer Learning?

- **Definition**: Transfer learning involves adapting a pretrained model to a specific task or domain using a smaller dataset.

- **Advantages**:

    o Reduces computational cost.

    o Enables training on limited data.

    o Leverages knowledge learned from large-scale datasets.

Steps for Transfer Learning

1. **Load a Pretrained Model**:

    o Use a model pretrained on a large, generic dataset.

    o Example: bert-base-uncased pretrained on general text.

2. **Fine-Tune on Specific Data**:

    o Modify the model's final layer for the new task.

    o Example: Replace a classification head with one suited for sentiment analysis.

3. **Optimize for the New Task**:

    o Use a task-specific dataset to fine-tune the model.

Code Example: Transfer Learning for Domain-Specific Fine-Tuning

python

```python
from transformers import AutoTokenizer,
AutoModelForSequenceClassification, Trainer, TrainingArguments
from datasets import load_dataset

# Load domain-specific dataset
dataset = load_dataset("financial_phrasebank")  # Example: Sentiment
analysis for financial text

# Tokenize the dataset
tokenizer = AutoTokenizer.from_pretrained("bert-base-uncased")
def preprocess(data):
    return tokenizer(data["text"], truncation=True,
padding="max_length", max_length=128)

encoded_dataset = dataset.map(preprocess, batched=True)

# Load pretrained BERT model
model = AutoModelForSequenceClassification.from_pretrained("bert-base-
uncased", num_labels=2)

# Define training arguments
training_args = TrainingArguments(
    output_dir="./results",
    evaluation_strategy="epoch",
    learning_rate=2e-5,
    per_device_train_batch_size=16,
    per_device_eval_batch_size=16,
    num_train_epochs=3,
    logging_dir="./logs",
)

# Create a Trainer
trainer = Trainer(
    model=model,
    args=training_args,
    train_dataset=encoded_dataset["train"],
    eval_dataset=encoded_dataset["test"],
    tokenizer=tokenizer,
)

# Fine-tune the model
trainer.train()
```

Exercise : Debug Training Convergence Issues with Small Datasets

Objective: Investigate and resolve issues when a model fails to converge on a small dataset.

Steps:

1. Load a small dataset and a pretrained model.

2. Check if the model converges during training.

3. Apply solutions like learning rate adjustment, regularization, or data augmentation.

Solution:

python

```
# Debugging Steps
# Step 1: Check learning rate
training_args = TrainingArguments(learning_rate=5e-5)  # Start with a
small learning rate

# Step 2: Add regularization
optimizer = optim.AdamW(model.parameters(), lr=5e-5,
weight_decay=0.01)

# Step 3: Apply data augmentation
def augment_data(data):
    data["text"] = data["text"].replace("good", "great")  # Example
augmentation
    return data

augmented_dataset = dataset.map(augment_data)
```

Summary

1. **Key Challenges**:

   o **Vanishing Gradients**: Addressed using ReLU, batch normalization, and residual connections.

   o **Overfitting**: Solved with dropout, regularization, and data augmentation.

   o **Long Training Times**: Reduced using mixed precision, gradient accumulation, and distributed training.

2. **Transfer Learning**:

- o   Adapt pretrained models to small datasets efficiently.

- o   Practical example demonstrated domain-specific fine-tuning.

3. **Debugging Training Issues**:

- o   Techniques to resolve convergence problems, including learning rate tuning and data augmentation.

This chapter equips you to tackle common obstacles in training LLMs effectively. Next, we'll explore deployment strategies for making LLMs production-ready.

Chapter 4: Deploying LLMs

Learning Objectives

By the end of this chapter, you will:

1. Understand the differences between real-time and batch inference and their trade-offs.

2. Learn how to optimize inference pipelines for low latency and high throughput.

3. Build a practical inference server using FastAPI for real-world deployment.

4. Practice testing and optimizing model latency.

4.1 Building Inference Pipelines

An inference pipeline is the backbone of deploying LLMs, enabling models to process inputs and deliver predictions efficiently. This section explores different inference modes, optimization strategies, and practical deployment techniques.

4.1.1 Real-Time vs. Batch Inference: Pros and Cons

Inference can occur in two main modes: **real-time (online)** and **batch (offline)**. The choice depends on the application and system requirements.

Real-Time Inference

- **Definition**: The model processes individual requests as they arrive and returns predictions immediately.

- **Use Cases**:

  o Chatbots and virtual assistants.

  o Real-time recommendation systems.

- **Advantages**:

  o Immediate response to user input.

  o Essential for interactive applications.

- **Challenges**:

  o Requires low latency for a seamless experience.

  o Can be resource-intensive with high request volumes.

Batch Inference

- **Definition**: The model processes multiple requests at once, usually at scheduled intervals.

- **Use Cases**:

  - Processing large datasets (e.g., summarizing thousands of documents).

  - Periodic analytics or report generation.

- **Advantages**:

  - Efficient resource utilization by processing requests in bulk.

  - Suitable for applications where immediacy is not critical.

- **Challenges**:

  - Introduces delays between request submission and result delivery.

Comparison Table

Feature	Real-Time Inference	Batch Inference
Latency	Low (milliseconds)	High (seconds to minutes)
Throughput	Handles single requests	Processes large batches
Use Cases	Interactive applications	Offline processing
Resource Efficiency	Lower for high traffic	Higher for bulk processing

4.1.2 Optimizing Inference Latency and Throughput

Efficient inference is critical for deploying LLMs in production. Here are key strategies:

1. Model Optimization

1. **Quantization**:

   - Convert model weights to lower precision (e.g., float32 $\rightarrow$ int8).

   - Reduces memory usage and speeds up inference.

   - Example: Use PyTorch's torch.quantization module.

2. **Pruning**:

   - Remove insignificant model parameters to reduce size.

o   Speeds up computations without significant loss in accuracy.

3. **Distillation**:

   o   Use a smaller student model trained to mimic the outputs of a larger teacher model.

   o   Example: DistilBERT is a distilled version of BERT.

2. Infrastructure Optimization

1. **Caching**:

   o   Cache frequent responses to reduce redundant computations.

   o   Example: Cache results of common queries in memory or a database.

2. **Load Balancing**:

   o   Distribute incoming requests across multiple servers to prevent bottlenecks.

   o   Tools: NGINX, AWS Elastic Load Balancer.

3. **Asynchronous Processing**:

   o   Use asynchronous frameworks (e.g., FastAPI) to handle requests efficiently.

Code Example: Build a FastAPI-Based Inference Server

Below is an implementation of an inference server using **FastAPI** to serve a pretrained model for real-time predictions.

Prerequisites

1.   Install required libraries:

bash

```
pip install fastapi uvicorn transformers torch
```

Code Implementation

python

```python
from fastapi import FastAPI, Request
from pydantic import BaseModel
from transformers import AutoTokenizer,
AutoModelForSequenceClassification
import torch

# Initialize FastAPI app
app = FastAPI()

# Load pretrained model and tokenizer
MODEL_NAME = "distilbert-base-uncased-finetuned-sst-2-english"  #
Sentiment analysis model
tokenizer = AutoTokenizer.from_pretrained(MODEL_NAME)
model = AutoModelForSequenceClassification.from_pretrained(MODEL_NAME)

# Define request and response schema
class InferenceRequest(BaseModel):
    text: str

class InferenceResponse(BaseModel):
    label: str
    confidence: float

# Inference route
@app.post("/predict", response_model=InferenceResponse)
async def predict(request: InferenceRequest):
    # Tokenize input text
    inputs = tokenizer(request.text, return_tensors="pt")

    # Perform inference
    with torch.no_grad():
        outputs = model(**inputs)
        logits = outputs.logits
        probabilities = torch.softmax(logits, dim=1)
        confidence, label_id = torch.max(probabilities, dim=1)

    # Convert label ID to human-readable label
    labels = ["Negative", "Positive"]
    return InferenceResponse(label=labels[label_id.item()],
confidence=confidence.item())

# Root endpoint
@app.get("/")
async def root():
    return {"message": "Welcome to the FastAPI-based inference
server!"}
```

Running the Server

1. Save the code in a file named app.py.

2. Start the server:

bash

```
uvicorn app:app --host 0.0.0.0 --port 8000
```

Testing the Server

1. Use curl or Postman to test:

bash

curl -X POST "http://127.0.0.1:8000/predict" -H "Content-Type: application/json" -d '{"text": "I love this product!"}'

2. **Expected Response**:

json

```
{
  "label": "Positive",
  "confidence": 0.99
}
```

Exercise : Deploy a FastAPI-Based Model and Test Latency

Objective: Deploy the FastAPI server and measure its response time for different inputs.

Steps:

1. Deploy the FastAPI server locally or on a cloud platform.

2. Use Python to send multiple requests and measure latency.

Solution:

python

```
import requests
import time

url = "http://127.0.0.1:8000/predict"
texts = ["This is amazing!", "I didn't like the movie.", "The weather
is nice today."]

for text in texts:
    start_time = time.time()
    response = requests.post(url, json={"text": text})
    latency = time.time() - start_time
    print(f"Input: {text}, Response: {response.json()}, Latency:
{latency:.4f} seconds")
```

Summary

1. **Real-Time vs. Batch Inference**:

   o Real-time inference is ideal for interactive applications, while batch
      inference is suited for bulk processing.

2. **Optimization Techniques**:

   o Techniques like quantization, pruning, and caching improve latency and
      throughput.

3. **Practical Deployment**:

   o The FastAPI example demonstrated how to deploy a sentiment analysis
      model for real-time predictions.

   o The exercise provided hands-on practice for measuring and optimizing
      latency.

With these tools and techniques, you are ready to deploy LLMs effectively in production environments. The next section will focus on strategies for ensuring security, reliability, and compliance in LLM deployment.

4.2 Deployment Strategies

Deploying Large Language Models (LLMs) efficiently requires careful consideration of containerization, orchestration, and deployment environments. This section explores deployment strategies, including Docker, Kubernetes, and the trade-offs between cloud-based and on-premises deployment.

4.2.1 Containerization with Docker and Orchestration with Kubernetes

What is Containerization?

Containerization packages an application and its dependencies into a portable unit (container) that can run consistently across different environments.

- **Tool**: Docker is the most popular tool for containerization.
- **Benefits**:
  - Environment consistency (development to production).
  - Simplified dependency management.
  - Portability across platforms.

What is Orchestration?

Orchestration manages the deployment, scaling, and operation of containers in production environments.

- **Tool**: Kubernetes is the most widely used container orchestration platform.
- **Benefits**:
  - Scalable deployments with automatic load balancing.
  - Resilience through self-healing and rolling updates.
  - Multi-node distribution for high availability.

Step-by-Step Deployment with Kubernetes

Objective: Deploy a FastAPI-based LLM inference application using Docker and Kubernetes.

1. Build and Containerize the Application

Dockerfile:

dockerfile

```
# Use an official Python image
FROM python:3.9-slim

# Set the working directory
WORKDIR /app
```

```
# Copy application files
COPY requirements.txt ./
COPY app.py ./

# Install dependencies
RUN pip install --no-cache-dir -r requirements.txt

# Expose the application port
EXPOSE 8000

# Start the FastAPI server
CMD ["uvicorn", "app:app", "--host", "0.0.0.0", "--port", "8000"]
```

Build and Tag the Docker Image:

bash

```bash
docker build -t llm-inference-app:latest .
```

Test the Docker Image Locally:

bash

```bash
docker run -p 8000:8000 llm-inference-app:latest
```

---

2. Write Kubernetes Deployment Configuration

k8s-deployment.yaml:

yaml

```yaml
apiVersion: apps/v1
kind: Deployment
metadata:
  name: llm-inference-app
spec:
  replicas: 3
  selector:
    matchLabels:
      app: llm-inference-app
  template:
    metadata:
      labels:
        app: llm-inference-app
    spec:
```

```yaml
      containers:
      - name: llm-inference-app
        image: llm-inference-app:latest
        ports:
        - containerPort: 8000
        resources:
          limits:
            memory: "512Mi"
            cpu: "500m"
---
apiVersion: v1
kind: Service
metadata:
  name: llm-inference-service
spec:
  selector:
    app: llm-inference-app
  ports:
  - protocol: TCP
    port: 80
    targetPort: 8000
  type: LoadBalancer
```

Key Components:

- **Deployment:**
  - Specifies the desired state of the application (e.g., 3 replicas).
  - Includes resource limits for memory and CPU.

- **Service:**
  - Exposes the application to external traffic via a LoadBalancer.

---

3. Deploy to Kubernetes

Steps:

1. Push the Docker image to a container registry (e.g., Docker Hub or AWS ECR):

bash

```bash
docker tag llm-inference-app:latest <your-dockerhub-username>/llm-inference-app:latest
docker push <your-dockerhub-username>/llm-inference-app:latest
```

2. Apply the Kubernetes configuration:

bash

```
kubectl apply -f k8s-deployment.yaml
```

3. Verify the deployment:

bash

```
kubectl get pods
kubectl get services
```

4. Test the service using the external IP:

bash

```
curl http://<external-ip>/predict -H "Content-Type: application/json"
-d '{"text": "I love FastAPI!"}'
```

Exercise : Containerize and Deploy a Small LLM Application

Objective: Containerize a FastAPI-based model and deploy it on a Kubernetes cluster.

Steps:

1. Write a Dockerfile and containerize the application.

2. Push the Docker image to a registry.

3. Write Kubernetes deployment and service configurations.

4. Deploy and test the application in a Kubernetes cluster.

4.2.2 Cloud vs. On-Premises Deployment: Cost and Resource Considerations

Cloud Deployment

Definition: Running applications on cloud infrastructure provided by platforms like AWS, Google Cloud, or Azure.

Benefits:

1. **Scalability**:

   o Resources can be scaled up or down dynamically.

   o Ideal for applications with fluctuating workloads.

2. **Managed Services**:

- Services like AWS Lambda, Google Cloud Run, and Azure Functions simplify deployment and scaling.

3. **Global Availability**:
   - Deploy applications closer to users via multiple regions.

Challenges:

- **Cost**:
  - Pay-as-you-go pricing can become expensive with high traffic.

- **Vendor Lock-In**:
  - Applications may rely on proprietary cloud services, making migration difficult.

On-Premises Deployment

Definition: Hosting applications on private servers within an organization's infrastructure.

Benefits:

1. **Control**:
   - Complete control over hardware, network, and security.
   - Suitable for industries with strict compliance requirements (e.g., healthcare, finance).

2. **Cost Efficiency**:
   - Avoids recurring cloud costs if infrastructure is already available.

Challenges:

- **Scalability**:
  - Limited by available hardware.

- **Maintenance**:
  - Requires in-house expertise for infrastructure management.

Comparison Table

Feature	Cloud Deployment	On-Premises Deployment
Scalability	High (elastic scaling)	Limited by available hardware
Cost	Pay-as-you-go, may increase with usage	High upfront investment
Security	Relies on cloud provider's security	Full control over security
Management	Provider-managed	Requires in-house management
Latency	May vary based on region	Typically low within private networks

Summary

1. **Containerization and Orchestration**:

   - Docker simplifies application packaging, and Kubernetes ensures scalable and reliable deployment.

   - The step-by-step example demonstrated deploying a FastAPI-based inference server.

2. **Cloud vs. On-Premises Deployment**:

   - Cloud deployment offers scalability and managed services but can be costly for high traffic.

   - On-premises deployment provides full control but requires significant expertise and resources.

By mastering these deployment strategies, you can choose the right approach for deploying LLMs based on your project's needs. In the next chapter, we will discuss optimizing LLMs for cost and performance at scale.

4.3 Security and Reliability

Deploying Large Language Models (LLMs) in production environments requires addressing critical aspects of **security** and **reliability** to ensure safe, abuse-resistant, and fault-tolerant operations. This chapter focuses on protecting LLM APIs from abuse and building robust inference pipelines.

4.3.1 Protecting LLM APIs from Abuse

APIs serving LLMs can be targets for abuse, including unauthorized usage, excessive requests, or malicious inputs. Protecting these APIs is essential to maintain operational efficiency and safeguard sensitive data.

Common Security Threats

1. **Unauthorized Access**:
   - Attackers may attempt to exploit the API without permission.
   - Example: Using stolen API keys to generate massive requests.

2. **Denial of Service (DoS) Attacks**:
   - Excessive requests may overload the server, causing service unavailability.

3. **Injection Attacks**:
   - Inputs designed to exploit vulnerabilities in the system.
   - Example: Sending malicious prompts to elicit undesirable model outputs.

4. **Data Leakage**:
   - APIs may inadvertently expose sensitive data through logs or responses.

Best Practices for API Security

1. Authentication and Authorization

- **API Keys**:
  - Require clients to include unique API keys in requests.
  - Use role-based access control to limit functionality (e.g., read-only vs. full access).

- **OAuth2**:
  - Implement OAuth2 for secure and scalable user authentication.

Code Example: Adding an API Key Middleware in FastAPI

python

```python
from fastapi import FastAPI, Request, HTTPException

app = FastAPI()
```

```
# Example API key
API_KEY = "mysecureapikey"

@app.middleware("http")
async def api_key_validator(request: Request, call_next):
    api_key = request.headers.get("x-api-key")
    if api_key != API_KEY:
        raise HTTPException(status_code=403, detail="Unauthorized")
    return await call_next(request)

@app.get("/")
async def root():
    return {"message": "Secure API"}
```

2. Rate Limiting

- **Purpose**: Prevent excessive or abusive requests.

- **Tools**: Libraries like slowapi for FastAPI or NGINX for server-side rate limiting.

Code Example: Implementing Rate Limiting with slowapi

python

```
from fastapi import FastAPI, HTTPException
from slowapi import Limiter
from slowapi.util import get_remote_address

app = FastAPI()
limiter = Limiter(key_func=get_remote_address)
app.state.limiter = limiter

@app.get("/")
@limiter.limit("5/minute")  # Limit to 5 requests per minute
async def root():
    return {"message": "Welcome to the rate-limited API!"}
```

3. Input Validation and Filtering

- **Sanitize Inputs**:
    - Check for malicious patterns in inputs (e.g., SQL injection-like syntax).

- **Prompt Restrictions**:
    - Restrict certain inputs that might cause unsafe or unethical model behavior.

Example:

python

```
@app.post("/predict")
async def predict(input: str):
    if "malicious_pattern" in input.lower():
        raise HTTPException(status_code=400, detail="Invalid input
detected")
    # Proceed with inference
```

4. Logging and Monitoring

- Track API usage and suspicious activity.
- Use tools like **Prometheus** and **Grafana** for real-time monitoring.

4.3.2 Building Fault-Tolerant Inference Pipelines

Why Fault Tolerance Matters

Inference pipelines must handle:

- **High Availability**: Ensuring continuous operation during hardware or software failures.
- **Resilience**: Recovering gracefully from unexpected errors.
- **Scalability**: Adapting to changes in traffic patterns.

Techniques for Fault-Tolerant Pipelines

1. Load Balancing

- Distribute traffic across multiple instances of the inference service.
- **Tools**:
  - NGINX: Lightweight and efficient for small setups.
  - Kubernetes: Built-in load balancing via services.

Example NGINX Configuration:

nginx

```
upstream llm_service {
    server app1.example.com;
    server app2.example.com;
    server app3.example.com;
}

server {
    listen 80;
    location / {
        proxy_pass http://llm_service;
    }
}
```

2. Redundancy

- Deploy multiple replicas of the model to ensure availability if one fails.
- **Implementation**: Kubernetes handles replicas and automatically restarts failed pods.

3. Circuit Breakers

- Temporarily block requests to a failing service to prevent cascading failures.
- **Tools**: Libraries like pybreaker in Python.

Code Example: Using pybreaker

python

```python
from pybreaker import CircuitBreaker

breaker = CircuitBreaker(fail_max=3, reset_timeout=60)

@breaker
def predict_with_resilience(input_text):
    # Call the inference service
    return model.predict(input_text)

try:
    response = predict_with_resilience("Sample input")
except CircuitBreakerError:
    print("Service is temporarily unavailable.")
```

4. Graceful Degradation

- Provide partial functionality when the primary system is unavailable.
- Example: Return cached responses or simpler predictions during outages.

5. Health Checks

- Regularly monitor the health of inference services.
- **Implementation**:
  - Add a /health endpoint to the API.
  - Use Kubernetes readiness and liveness probes.

Code Example: Health Endpoint

python

```
@app.get("/health")
async def health():
    return {"status": "ok"}
Kubernetes Probe Configuration:
yaml

livenessProbe:
  httpGet:
    path: /health
    port: 8000
  initialDelaySeconds: 5
  periodSeconds: 10
```

Examples of Fault-Tolerant Architectures

Feature	Implementation
Redundancy	Deploy multiple replicas in Kubernetes
Auto-Scaling	Horizontal Pod Autoscaler (HPA) for traffic spikes
Monitoring	Prometheus for metrics, Grafana for visualization
Failover	Use fallback services for degraded functionality

Summary

1. **Protecting LLM APIs**:

- Techniques like API keys, rate limiting, and input validation safeguard against abuse.

- Tools such as slowapi and pybreaker enhance security and resilience.

2. **Building Fault-Tolerant Pipelines**:

- Strategies like load balancing, redundancy, and health checks ensure high availability.

- Practical examples demonstrated robust setups using FastAPI, Kubernetes, and NGINX.

With secure and fault-tolerant pipelines, your LLM deployment is equipped to handle production challenges effectively. The next chapter will focus on scaling LLMs to handle increasing demands efficiently.

Chapter 5: Scaling and Optimizing LLMs

Learning Objectives

By the end of this chapter, you will:

1. Understand and compare horizontal scaling and vertical scaling strategies for deploying LLMs.

2. Learn about elastic scaling in cloud environments for cost efficiency and performance.

3. Explore practical examples and architectures for scaling LLMs.

5.1 Scaling Strategies

Scaling Large Language Models (LLMs) is essential to handle increasing workloads and ensure seamless performance. Scaling strategies can be broadly classified into **horizontal scaling** and **vertical scaling**.

5.1.1 Horizontal Scaling vs. Vertical Scaling

Horizontal Scaling

Definition:
Adding more machines (or instances) to distribute the workload.

- **How It Works**:
    - Multiple replicas of the application are deployed, each capable of handling part of the traffic.
    - A load balancer distributes incoming requests across these instances.

- **Advantages**:
    - Virtually unlimited scalability.
    - Increased fault tolerance: If one instance fails, others can continue serving requests.
    - No upper limit imposed by a single machine's capacity.

- **Challenges**:
    - Requires a load balancing mechanism.
    - Data consistency issues in stateful applications.

Example Architecture:

plaintext

```
+--------------------+
|   Load Balancer    |
+--------------------+
     /   |   \
+-------+ +-------+ +-------+
| Node 1| | Node 2| | Node 3|
+-------+ +-------+ +-------+
```

Vertical Scaling

Definition:
Increasing the resources (e.g., CPU, RAM) of a single machine to handle larger workloads.

- **How It Works**:
    - Upgrade the hardware of the existing instance instead of adding more machines.
    - Suitable for stateful applications or legacy systems.

- **Advantages**:
    - Simpler implementation.
    - No changes needed in application architecture.

- **Challenges**:
    - Limited by the maximum capacity of a single machine.
    - Downtime may occur during hardware upgrades.

Example: Upgrading from a 4-core CPU machine with 16GB RAM to an 8-core CPU machine with 32GB RAM.

Comparison of Horizontal and Vertical Scaling

Feature	Horizontal Scaling	Vertical Scaling
Scalability	High (can add more machines)	Limited (hardware constraints)
Fault Tolerance	High (redundancy)	Low (single point of failure)
Implementation	Complex (requires load balancing)	Simple (upgrade existing instance)
Cost Efficiency	High at scale	Expensive for high resource tiers

Code Example: Implementing Load Balancing for Horizontal Scaling with NGINX

nginx

```
upstream llm_cluster {
    server node1.example.com;
    server node2.example.com;
    server node3.example.com;
}

server {
    listen 80;

    location / {
        proxy_pass http://llm_cluster;
        proxy_set_header Host $host;
    }
}
```

How It Works:

1. Incoming traffic is distributed among node1, node2, and node3.

2. Each node runs an instance of the LLM inference service.

5.1.2 Elastic Scaling in Cloud Environments

Definition:
Elastic scaling allows resources to scale up or down automatically based on demand. This feature is commonly provided by cloud platforms like AWS, Azure, and Google Cloud.

Benefits of Elastic Scaling

1. **Cost Efficiency**:
   - Pay only for the resources you use.
   - Scale down during off-peak hours to save costs.

2. **Dynamic Resource Allocation**:
   - Automatically handle traffic spikes without manual intervention.

3. **Global Availability**:
   - Deploy applications across multiple regions and scale them independently.

How Elastic Scaling Works

1. **Monitoring**:
   - Cloud platforms monitor metrics like CPU usage, memory utilization, and request rates.

2. **Scaling Decision**:
   - Based on predefined thresholds, the system decides whether to add or remove instances.

3. **Execution**:
   - Additional instances are provisioned or existing ones are terminated automatically.

Examples of Elastic Scaling in Major Cloud Platforms

Platform	Elastic Scaling Service	Features
AWS	Auto Scaling Groups (ASG)	Scales EC2 instances based on target metrics
Google Cloud	Autoscaler	Scales Compute Engine VMs
Microsoft Azure	Virtual Machine Scale Sets	Manages VM pools with automatic scaling
Kubernetes	Horizontal Pod Autoscaler (HPA)	Scales pods based on CPU or custom metrics

Elastic Scaling Architecture

Scenario: Scaling an LLM API based on CPU usage.

1. **Cloud Watcher**:
   - Monitors metrics like CPU usage and request latency.

2. **Autoscaler**:
   - Adds or removes instances based on predefined thresholds.

3. **Load Balancer**:
   - Distributes traffic among all available instances.

Example Architecture:

plaintext

```
+----------------------+
|   Load Balancer   |
+----------------------+
     /     \
+-------+   +-------+
| VM 1 |   | VM 2 | (Autoscaled)
+-------+   +-------+
```

Code Example: Configuring AWS Auto Scaling Group

yaml

```yaml
Resources:
 AutoScalingGroup:
  Type: AWS::AutoScaling::AutoScalingGroup
  Properties:
   MinSize: 2
   MaxSize: 10
```

DesiredCapacity: 3

LaunchConfigurationName: MyLaunchConfig

AvailabilityZones:

  - us-east-1a

  - us-east-1b

TargetGroupARNs:

  - !Ref MyTargetGroup

MetricsCollection:

  - Granularity: "1Minute"

Tags:

  - Key: Name

    Value: llm-instance

    PropagateAtLaunch: true

Explanation:

1. The Auto Scaling Group maintains a minimum of 2 instances and scales up to 10 based on demand.

2. Instances are distributed across availability zones for redundancy.

Exercise : Implement Elastic Scaling with Kubernetes

Objective: Deploy a Kubernetes-based LLM inference service with automatic scaling.

Steps:

1. Enable Kubernetes **Horizontal Pod Autoscaler (HPA)**.

2. Set up CPU-based scaling rules.

Solution:

1. Deploy the application:

bash

```
kubectl apply -f deployment.yaml
```
2. Enable HPA:

bash

```
kubectl autoscale deployment llm-inference-deployment --cpu-percent=50 --min=2 --max=10
```

3. Monitor scaling:

bash

```
kubectl get hpa
```

Summary

1. **Horizontal vs. Vertical Scaling**:

   o Horizontal scaling adds machines to handle more requests.

   o Vertical scaling upgrades hardware for a single machine.

2. **Elastic Scaling**:

   o Cloud-based elastic scaling dynamically adjusts resources to meet demand.

   o Tools like AWS Auto Scaling Groups and Kubernetes HPA simplify the process.

3. **Hands-On Practice**:

   o NGINX-based load balancing and Kubernetes HPA examples provided practical insights into scaling strategies.

By mastering these scaling techniques, you can ensure that your LLM deployments handle increasing demands efficiently while minimizing costs. The next section will focus on optimizing LLMs for performance and resource efficiency.

5.2 Optimization Techniques

Optimizing Large Language Models (LLMs) is essential to reduce resource consumption, improve inference speed, and make deployment more cost-effective. This section focuses on two powerful optimization techniques: **model compression** (quantization and pruning) and **knowledge distillation**.

5.2.1 Model Compression: Quantization and Pruning

What is Model Compression?

Model compression reduces the size of a model while retaining its accuracy, making it more efficient for inference. This is achieved using techniques like **quantization** and **pruning**.

Quantization

Definition:

Quantization reduces the precision of model parameters (weights) and activations from higher precision (e.g., 32-bit floating point) to lower precision (e.g., 8-bit integers).

Benefits:

1. Reduces model size significantly.

2. Decreases memory bandwidth requirements.

3. Improves inference speed on hardware optimized for low precision (e.g., NVIDIA Tensor Cores, CPUs with AVX-512).

Types of Quantization:

1. **Post-Training Quantization**:

   o Applies quantization after training without retraining the model.

   o Example: TensorFlow Lite supports post-training quantization.

2. **Quantization-Aware Training (QAT)**:

   o Simulates quantization during training to improve accuracy of the quantized model.

   o Example: Supported in PyTorch.

Code Example: Quantizing a Model for Efficient Inference

Below is a PyTorch implementation of post-training quantization for a pretrained BERT model.

python

```
import torch
```

```
from transformers import AutoModelForSequenceClassification,
AutoTokenizer

# Load pretrained BERT model and tokenizer
model_name = "distilbert-base-uncased-finetuned-sst-2-english"
model = AutoModelForSequenceClassification.from_pretrained(model_name)
tokenizer = AutoTokenizer.from_pretrained(model_name)

# Quantize the model
quantized_model = torch.quantization.quantize_dynamic(
    model, {torch.nn.Linear}, dtype=torch.qint8
)

# Test the quantized model
text = "This is an amazing optimization technique!"
inputs = tokenizer(text, return_tensors="pt")
outputs = quantized_model(**inputs)
```

print("Quantized Model Output:", outputs.logits)

Expected Outcome:

- Model size is reduced, and inference speed is faster compared to the original model.

Pruning

Definition:

Pruning removes insignificant weights or neurons from a model, reducing its size and computation requirements.

Types of Pruning:

1. **Unstructured Pruning**:

   o Removes individual weights below a certain threshold.

   o Example: Setting weights close to zero as zero.

2. **Structured Pruning**:

   o Removes entire neurons, filters, or layers.

   o Example: Removing a convolutional layer.

Code Example: Pruning a Model in PyTorch

Below is an example of applying unstructured pruning.

python

```
import torch.nn.utils.prune as prune

# Define a simple model
model = torch.nn.Linear(10, 5)

# Apply pruning
prune.random_unstructured(model, name="weight", amount=0.3)

# Check pruned weights
print("Pruned Model Weights:", model.weight)
```

Comparison: Quantization vs. Pruning

Feature	Quantization	Pruning
Primary Goal	Reduce precision	Remove insignificant weights
Impact on Model	Smaller data type size	Smaller model size
Effectiveness	Better for hardware optimization	Reduces memory and computational load

5.2.2 Knowledge Distillation: Training Smaller Models with Comparable Performance

What is Knowledge Distillation?

Knowledge distillation trains a smaller **student model** to mimic the behavior of a larger **teacher model**, transferring the knowledge of the teacher to the student.

How It Works:

1. **Teacher Model**:

   o A large, pretrained model generates soft labels (probability distributions) for the training data.

2. **Student Model**:

   o A smaller model is trained to reproduce the teacher's soft labels.

3. **Loss Function**:

- Combines standard cross-entropy loss (hard labels) and Kullback-Leibler divergence (soft labels).

Benefits of Knowledge Distillation:

1. Smaller model size.

2. Faster inference.

3. Comparable performance to the teacher model on specific tasks.

Code Example: Implementing Knowledge Distillation in PyTorch

Below is an implementation of knowledge distillation using a teacher and student model.

python

```python
import torch
import torch.nn as nn
from transformers import AutoModelForSequenceClassification,
AutoTokenizer

# Load teacher and student models
teacher_model =
AutoModelForSequenceClassification.from_pretrained("bert-base-
uncased", num_labels=2)
student_model =
AutoModelForSequenceClassification.from_pretrained("distilbert-base-
uncased", num_labels=2)

# Define tokenizer
tokenizer = AutoTokenizer.from_pretrained("bert-base-uncased")

# Define loss function
loss_fn = nn.KLDivLoss(reduction="batchmean")

# Sample input text
text = "Knowledge distillation reduces model size."
inputs = tokenizer(text, return_tensors="pt")

# Teacher model output
teacher_logits = teacher_model(**inputs).logits

# Student model output
```

```
student_logits = student_model(**inputs).logits

# Calculate soft targets
teacher_soft_targets = torch.softmax(teacher_logits / 2.0, dim=-1)
student_soft_targets = torch.log_softmax(student_logits / 2.0, dim=-1)

# Compute distillation loss
distillation_loss = loss_fn(student_soft_targets,
teacher_soft_targets)
print("Distillation Loss:", distillation_loss.item())
```

Exercise : Compare Inference Speed and Accuracy of Compressed vs. Original Models

Objective: Compare the performance of a quantized model and an original model in terms of speed and accuracy.

Steps:

1. Load a pretrained model and apply quantization.

2. Measure inference time and accuracy on a test dataset for both models.

3. Compare the results.

Code for Comparison:

python

```
import time
from datasets import load_dataset
from transformers import AutoModelForSequenceClassification,
AutoTokenizer

# Load original and quantized models
original_model =
AutoModelForSequenceClassification.from_pretrained("bert-base-
uncased", num_labels=2)
quantized_model = torch.quantization.quantize_dynamic(
    original_model, {torch.nn.Linear}, dtype=torch.qint8
)

tokenizer = AutoTokenizer.from_pretrained("bert-base-uncased")

# Load dataset
dataset = load_dataset("imdb", split="test[:100]")

# Define a function to measure inference time
```

```python
def measure_inference_time(model, text):
    inputs = tokenizer(text, return_tensors="pt")
    start_time = time.time()
    outputs = model(**inputs)
    elapsed_time = time.time() - start_time
    return elapsed_time, torch.argmax(outputs.logits).item()

# Compare models
original_time, original_pred = measure_inference_time(original_model,
"The movie was fantastic!")
quantized_time, quantized_pred =
measure_inference_time(quantized_model, "The movie was fantastic!")

print(f"Original Model - Time: {original_time:.4f}s, Prediction:
{original_pred}")
print(f"Quantized Model - Time: {quantized_time:.4f}s, Prediction:
{quantized_pred}")
```

Summary

1. **Model Compression**:

   o Quantization and pruning reduce model size and speed up inference.

   o Practical examples demonstrated both techniques in PyTorch.

2. **Knowledge Distillation**:

   o Smaller models can achieve near-teacher-level performance by mimicking a larger model.

   o PyTorch implementation showed how to calculate distillation loss.

3. **Hands-On Comparison**:

   o The exercise provided a method to evaluate speed and accuracy differences between compressed and original models.

With these optimization techniques, you can deploy resource-efficient LLMs without compromising performance. The next chapter will focus on real-world applications and case studies of LLMs.

5.3 Cost Optimization

Cost optimization is critical when working with Large Language Models (LLMs), especially given their resource-intensive nature for both training and inference. This section delves into strategies to minimize compute costs without sacrificing performance, including best practices for managing expenses during training and inference.

5.3.1 Managing Compute Costs for Training and Inference

Why Focus on Cost Optimization?

- **Training Costs**: Training large-scale models on vast datasets can incur significant expenses, particularly on cloud platforms.

- **Inference Costs**: Even after deployment, high traffic or suboptimal configurations can lead to ongoing operational costs.

By implementing strategic optimizations, you can significantly reduce both training and inference costs while maintaining efficiency.

Cost Optimization During Training

1. Use Pretrained Models

- **Why**: Training a model from scratch is expensive and time-consuming.

- **How**: Use models like bert-base-uncased or gpt-3 as starting points and fine-tune them for specific tasks.

2. Distributed Training

- Split the workload across multiple GPUs or nodes for faster training.

- Use **spot instances** or **preemptible VMs** to leverage discounted cloud compute rates.

Example: Using AWS Spot Instances

bash

```
aws ec2 run-instances \
  --instance-type p3.2xlarge \
  --instance-market-options '{"MarketType": "spot"}' \
  --image-id ami-0abcdef1234567890
```

3. Mixed-Precision Training

- Reduces memory usage and accelerates computation by using lower precision (e.g., float16) instead of float32.

Code Example: PyTorch AMP for Mixed-Precision Training

python

```
from torch.cuda.amp import GradScaler, autocast

scaler = GradScaler()

for epoch in range(epochs):
    for inputs, labels in dataloader:
        optimizer.zero_grad()
        with autocast():   # Use mixed precision
            outputs = model(inputs)
            loss = criterion(outputs, labels)
        scaler.scale(loss).backward()
        scaler.step(optimizer)
        scaler.update()
```

4. Efficient Data Loading

- Use **data caching** and optimized data pipelines to avoid bottlenecks.

- Frameworks like **tf.data** and **PyTorch DataLoader** support parallel data loading.

5. Spotting Inefficiencies in Hyperparameter Tuning

- Use **hyperparameter optimization frameworks** like Optuna or Ray Tune to automate parameter search.

- Focus on critical parameters (e.g., learning rate, batch size) to minimize trial-and-error cycles.

Code Example: Hyperparameter Tuning with Optuna

python

```
import optuna

def objective(trial):
    learning_rate = trial.suggest_loguniform("learning_rate", 1e-5,
1e-1)
    batch_size = trial.suggest_categorical("batch_size", [16, 32, 64])

    # Train model with suggested parameters
    accuracy = train_model(learning_rate, batch_size)
    return accuracy

study = optuna.create_study(direction="maximize")
study.optimize(objective, n_trials=50)
print(study.best_params)
```

Cost Optimization During Inference

1. Optimize Model Size

- Use techniques like **quantization**, **pruning**, or **knowledge distillation** to deploy smaller, efficient models.

2. Use Scalable Infrastructure

- Use serverless architectures (e.g., AWS Lambda, Google Cloud Functions) for event-driven workloads.

- Use **Horizontal Pod Autoscaler (HPA)** in Kubernetes for automatic scaling during high traffic.

3. Batch Inference for Bulk Requests

- Combine multiple inference requests into a single batch to utilize hardware efficiently.

Code Example: Batch Inference with PyTorch

python

```
batch = tokenizer(["Input 1", "Input 2", "Input 3"],
return_tensors="pt", padding=True)
outputs = model(**batch)
print(outputs.logits)
```

4. Cache Frequent Results

- Use in-memory caching (e.g., Redis) to store frequent or predictable responses, reducing redundant computations.

Code Example: Using Redis for Caching

python

```
import redis

# Connect to Redis
cache = redis.Redis(host='localhost', port=6379, db=0)

def get_prediction(input_text):
    # Check cache
    if cache.exists(input_text):
        return cache.get(input_text).decode()

    # Compute prediction
```

```
prediction = model.predict(input_text)
cache.set(input_text, prediction)  # Store result in cache
return prediction
```

5. Use Cost-Aware Cloud Features

- **AWS Savings Plans**: Commit to consistent usage for reduced rates.

- **Reserved Instances**: Purchase reserved capacity for predictable workloads.

Comparison: Cost-Saving Techniques for Training vs. Inference

Technique	Training	Inference
Pretrained Models	Fine-tune instead of training from scratch	Not applicable
Mixed Precision	Speeds up training	Reduces inference latency
Caching	Not applicable	Saves computation for frequent queries
Batch Processing	Data batching in GPUs	Combines multiple requests
Scalable Infrastructure	Distributed training	Autoscaling for dynamic workloads

Case Study: Cost Optimization for an LLM Deployment

Scenario: A company uses a BERT-based model for text summarization and faces high operational costs.

1. **Initial Setup**:
   - Training on cloud GPUs without spot instances.
   - Running a full-sized model for inference on dedicated servers.

2. **Optimizations Applied**:
   - Used pretrained bert-base-uncased and fine-tuned it on a summarization dataset.
   - Quantized the model to reduce inference latency and memory usage.
   - Migrated to Kubernetes with HPA for elastic scaling.
   - Cached frequent requests using Redis.

3. **Results**:

   o **Training Costs**: Reduced by 40% using spot instances and mixed precision.

   o **Inference Costs**: Reduced by 60% with quantization and caching.

   o **Scalability**: Handled a 5x increase in traffic seamlessly with HPA.

Summary

1. **Training Optimization**:

   o Use pretrained models, mixed precision, and distributed training for cost-effective training.

   o Employ hyperparameter tuning tools to streamline experimentation.

2. **Inference Optimization**:

   o Techniques like quantization, caching, and batch inference minimize costs.

   o Scalable and serverless architectures dynamically adjust to traffic demands.

3. **Hands-On Practice**:

   o Code examples demonstrated practical ways to implement cost-saving strategies for both training and inference.

By applying these strategies, you can significantly reduce operational costs, making LLM deployments more sustainable and efficient. In the next chapter, we will explore real-world applications of LLMs, illustrating how they drive value across industries.

Chapter 6: Real-World Applications of LLMs

Large Language Models (LLMs) are versatile tools with applications across various industries. In this chapter, we explore industry-specific use cases such as chatbots, virtual assistants, summarization, and sentiment analysis. Practical examples and code implementations illustrate how to harness LLMs for real-world challenges.

6.1 Industry-Specific Use Cases

6.1.1 Chatbots and Virtual Assistants

Overview

- **Chatbots**: Automated conversational agents that assist users by responding to queries.
- **Virtual Assistants**: Advanced systems capable of carrying out tasks, providing information, and managing schedules.

Applications:

- **Customer Support**:
    o Automating responses to frequently asked questions.
    o Reducing workload on human agents.
- **Healthcare**:
    o Assisting patients with preliminary diagnoses or appointment scheduling.
- **E-Commerce**:
    o Product recommendations and personalized shopping experiences.

Code: Build a Chatbot Using GPT and Flask

The following implementation demonstrates how to create a chatbot using OpenAI's GPT model and Flask for the API backend.

Prerequisites:

1. Install required libraries:

bash

```bash
pip install openai flask
```

Code Implementation:

python

```python
from flask import Flask, request, jsonify
import openai

# Initialize Flask app
app = Flask(__name__)

# OpenAI API Key
openai.api_key = "your_openai_api_key"

@app.route("/chat", methods=["POST"])
def chat():
    user_input = request.json.get("message", "")
    if not user_input:
        return jsonify({"error": "Message cannot be empty"}), 400

    try:
        # Generate response using GPT
        response = openai.Completion.create(
            engine="text-davinci-003",  # Choose your GPT model
            prompt=f"User: {user_input}\nBot:",
            max_tokens=150,
            n=1,
            stop=None,
            temperature=0.7,
        )
        bot_reply = response["choices"][0]["text"].strip()
        return jsonify({"reply": bot_reply})
    except Exception as e:
        return jsonify({"error": str(e)}), 500

# Start the Flask server
if __name__ == "__main__":
    app.run(host="0.0.0.0", port=5000)
```

How It Works:

1. The Flask server receives a user's input via a POST request.

2. The input is passed to GPT, which generates a response.

3. The response is returned as JSON to the user.

Test the Chatbot:

1. Start the server:

bash

```
python app.py
```

2. Send a test request:

bash

```
curl -X POST "http://127.0.0.1:5000/chat" -H "Content-Type:
application/json" -d '{"message": "What is the weather today?"}'
```

6.1.2 Summarization and Sentiment Analysis

Overview

1. **Summarization:**

   o Reduces long texts into concise summaries while retaining key information.

   o Applications:

     ▪ Summarizing news articles, legal documents, or research papers.

2. **Sentiment Analysis:**

   o Identifies the sentiment (e.g., positive, negative, neutral) in text.

   o Applications:

     ▪ Monitoring customer feedback and social media sentiment.

Code: Fine-Tune a Model for Text Summarization

Prerequisites:

1. Install required libraries:

bash

```
pip install transformers datasets
```

Steps:

1. Use a pretrained model like t5-small for summarization.

2. Fine-tune the model on a custom dataset (e.g., CNN/Daily Mail).

Code Implementation:

python

```python
from datasets import load_dataset
from transformers import T5Tokenizer, T5ForConditionalGeneration,
Trainer, TrainingArguments

# Load a dataset
dataset = load_dataset("cnn_dailymail", "3.0.0")

# Load tokenizer and model
model_name = "t5-small"
tokenizer = T5Tokenizer.from_pretrained(model_name)
model = T5ForConditionalGeneration.from_pretrained(model_name)

# Preprocess the dataset
def preprocess(data):
    inputs = ["summarize: " + text for text in data["article"]]
    targets = data["highlights"]
    model_inputs = tokenizer(inputs, max_length=512, truncation=True,
padding="max_length")
    labels = tokenizer(targets, max_length=150, truncation=True,
padding="max_length").input_ids
    model_inputs["labels"] = labels
    return model_inputs

tokenized_dataset = dataset.map(preprocess, batched=True)

# Define training arguments
training_args = TrainingArguments(
    output_dir="./results",
    evaluation_strategy="epoch",
    learning_rate=2e-5,
    per_device_train_batch_size=8,
    per_device_eval_batch_size=8,
```

```
        num_train_epochs=3,
        weight_decay=0.01,
        save_total_limit=1,
        save_steps=500,
)

# Train the model
trainer = Trainer(
        model=model,
        args=training_args,
        train_dataset=tokenized_dataset["train"],
        eval_dataset=tokenized_dataset["validation"],
        tokenizer=tokenizer,
)

trainer.train()
```

How It Works:

1. The dataset (cnn_dailymail) contains news articles and corresponding summaries.

2. The model is fine-tuned using the T5 architecture, which is optimized for text-to-text tasks.

Exercise : Build a Custom Summarization Tool for News Articles

Objective: Create a summarization tool that accepts raw news articles and generates summaries.

Steps:

1. Fine-tune a T5 model on a dataset of news articles.

2. Deploy the model using FastAPI or Flask for an interactive interface.

Solution Code:

python

```
from fastapi import FastAPI, Request
from transformers import T5Tokenizer, T5ForConditionalGeneration

# Initialize FastAPI app
app = FastAPI()

# Load fine-tuned model and tokenizer
```

```
model_name = "t5-small"
tokenizer = T5Tokenizer.from_pretrained(model_name)
model = T5ForConditionalGeneration.from_pretrained("./results")  #
Path to fine-tuned model

@app.post("/summarize")
async def summarize(request: Request):
    data = await request.json()
    article = data.get("article", "")
    if not article:
        return {"error": "Article cannot be empty"}

    # Generate summary
    inputs = tokenizer("summarize: " + article, return_tensors="pt",
max_length=512, truncation=True)
    summary_ids = model.generate(inputs["input_ids"], max_length=150,
min_length=40, length_penalty=2.0, num_beams=4)
    summary = tokenizer.decode(summary_ids[0],
skip_special_tokens=True)
    return {"summary": summary}

# Run the server
if __name__ == "__main__":
    import uvicorn
    uvicorn.run(app, host="0.0.0.0", port=8000)
```

Summary

1. **Chatbots and Virtual Assistants**:

   o Practical implementation using GPT and Flask illustrated how to build interactive chatbots.

   o Applications include customer support, healthcare, and e-commerce.

2. **Summarization and Sentiment Analysis**:

   o Summarization reduces lengthy text into concise summaries.

   o Sentiment analysis identifies emotions in text, aiding customer feedback analysis.

3. **Hands-On Exercise**:

   o Readers practiced building a custom summarization tool for news articles.

By applying these techniques, you can create impactful applications that leverage the full potential of LLMs across industries. The next chapter will focus on maintaining and monitoring LLMs in production environments.

6.2 Advanced Applications

In this section, we explore advanced applications of Large Language Models (LLMs) in **creative writing and content generation** and delve into the exciting domain of **multimodal AI**, where text interacts seamlessly with images and audio. These applications demonstrate the versatility and potential of LLMs beyond traditional use cases.

6.2.1 Creative Writing and Content Generation

Overview

LLMs can generate engaging and human-like text for creative purposes such as:

- Writing stories, poems, or scripts.
- Crafting marketing copy and personalized content.
- Generating educational or training materials.

Applications of Creative Writing

1. **Storytelling**:
   - Generate fiction or non-fiction narratives based on prompts.
   - Assist authors with idea generation and plot development.
2. **Marketing and Copywriting**:
   - Create ad campaigns, taglines, and personalized email content.
   - Example: Crafting engaging product descriptions for e-commerce.
3. **Educational Content**:
   - Produce tutorials, summaries, and interactive learning materials.

Code Example: Story Generation with GPT

Objective: Use GPT to generate a short story based on a user-provided prompt.

Code Implementation:

python

```
import openai
```

```
# OpenAI API Key
openai.api_key = "your_openai_api_key"

# Function to generate a story
def generate_story(prompt, max_tokens=300):
    response = openai.Completion.create(
        engine="text-davinci-003",
        prompt=f"Write a short story based on the following
prompt:\n{prompt}\n",
        max_tokens=max_tokens,
        temperature=0.8,
        n=1,
        stop=None,
    )
    return response["choices"][0]["text"].strip()

# Example usage
prompt = "A lonely robot exploring a distant planet discovers
something unexpected."
story = generate_story(prompt)
print("Generated Story:\n", story)
```

How It Works:

1. The user provides a creative prompt.

2. The GPT model generates a story, controlling output length and creativity through parameters like max_tokens and temperature.

Output Example:

less

Generated Story:

Once upon a time, on a barren planet far from Earth, a lonely robot named Exo wandered aimlessly...

Challenges and Solutions in Creative Writing:

1. **Challenge**: Lack of originality.

   o **Solution**: Introduce randomness using the temperature parameter to add creative variation.

2. **Challenge**: Content alignment.

- o **Solution**: Fine-tune the model on specific genres or writing styles.

6.2.2 Multimodal AI: Text, Image, and Audio Applications

Overview

Multimodal AI enables models to process and generate content across different modalities (e.g., text, images, and audio). This capability is essential for applications requiring a combination of sensory inputs or outputs.

Applications of Multimodal AI

1. **Text-to-Image Generation**:
   - o Generate images from descriptive text prompts.
   - o Example: Tools like DALL-E generate art based on textual instructions.

2. **Visual Question Answering (VQA)**:
   - o Answer questions about images by analyzing both visual and textual inputs.
   - o Example: "What color is the car in this picture?"

3. **Audio-Text Integration**:
   - o Transcribe speech to text and generate contextual responses.
   - o Example: Real-time speech assistants like Alexa or Siri.

4. **Content Creation**:
   - o Combine modalities for creative projects like illustrated books or animated stories.

Code Example: Text-to-Image Generation Using OpenAI's DALL-E

Objective: Generate an image from a textual description.

Code Implementation:

python

```
import openai
```

```
# OpenAI API Key
openai.api_key = "your_openai_api_key"

# Function to generate an image from text
def generate_image(prompt):
    response = openai.Image.create(
        prompt=prompt,
        n=1,
        size="512x512"
    )
    return response["data"][0]["url"]

# Example usage
prompt = "A futuristic cityscape at sunset with flying cars"
image_url = generate_image(prompt)
print("Generated Image URL:", image_url)
```

Output:

- A link to the generated image, e.g., https://openai.com/.../image.png.

Code Example: Multimodal Input for Visual Question Answering (VQA)

Objective: Answer questions about an image using a pretrained multimodal model.

Code Implementation:

python

```
from transformers import BlipProcessor, BlipForQuestionAnswering
from PIL import Image

# Load model and processor
processor = BlipProcessor.from_pretrained("Salesforce/blip-vqa-base")
model = BlipForQuestionAnswering.from_pretrained("Salesforce/blip-vqa-base")

# Load an image
image = Image.open("example_image.jpg")

# Prepare inputs
question = "What is the color of the car?"
inputs = processor(image, question, return_tensors="pt")

# Get model output
```

```
outputs = model.generate(**inputs)
answer = processor.decode(outputs[0], skip_special_tokens=True)
print("Answer:", answer)
```

How It Works:

1. The user provides an image and a related question.

2. The BLIP model processes the visual and textual inputs to generate an answer.

Example Output:

vbnet

Answer: The car is red.

Challenges and Solutions in Multimodal AI:

1. **Challenge**: High computational requirements.

   - **Solution**: Use model optimization techniques like quantization for efficient inference.

2. **Challenge**: Data alignment.

   - **Solution**: Use high-quality paired datasets (e.g., text-image datasets like MS COCO).

Summary

1. **Creative Writing and Content Generation**:

   - LLMs can generate compelling stories, marketing content, and educational materials.

   - Practical example: Story generation with GPT demonstrated the ease of creating engaging narratives.

2. **Multimodal AI Applications**:

   - Combining text, image, and audio capabilities opens possibilities for advanced applications like text-to-image generation and visual question answering.

   - Practical examples illustrated how to integrate these modalities using tools like DALL-E and BLIP.

3. **Hands-On Practice**:

- o Code examples provided a foundation for experimenting with creative and multimodal AI projects.

This chapter demonstrated the innovative potential of LLMs in advanced applications. The next chapter will cover strategies for maintaining and monitoring LLMs in production environments to ensure reliability and performance.

6.3 Case Studies

Case studies offer valuable insights into real-world applications of Large Language Models (LLMs) across industries. In this section, we explore two in-depth case studies: using GPT for customer support automation and fine-tuning models for domain-specific tasks. These examples demonstrate how to overcome challenges and maximize the potential of LLMs.

Case Study 1: Using GPT for Customer Support Automation

Problem Statement

A retail company receives thousands of customer support queries daily, ranging from order status inquiries to troubleshooting product issues. The existing support team struggles to handle this volume, resulting in delays and customer dissatisfaction.

Solution

The company implemented GPT-based chatbots to automate responses to frequently asked questions (FAQs) while escalating complex queries to human agents.

Implementation Steps

1. Data Collection and Preparation

- **Source Data**:
    - o Historical chat logs and FAQ databases.
    - o Categorized queries into common topics (e.g., order tracking, returns, product info).
- **Preprocessing**:
    - o Cleaned the data by removing irrelevant information (e.g., timestamps, agent IDs).
    - o Standardized query formats for consistency.

2. Fine-Tuning GPT for Support

- **Model Choice**:
  - Used text-davinci-003 from OpenAI for its advanced understanding of conversational contexts.

- **Fine-Tuning Dataset**:
  - Created a dataset of input-output pairs:
    - Input: Customer queries (e.g., "Where is my order?")
    - Output: Corresponding responses (e.g., "Your order is on the way and will arrive by [date].").

Code Example:

python

```python
import openai

# OpenAI API Key
openai.api_key = "your_openai_api_key"

# Sample fine-tuning data
data = [
    {"prompt": "Where is my order?\n", "completion": "Your order is on
its way and will arrive by tomorrow.\n"},
    {"prompt": "How do I return an item?\n", "completion": "You can
initiate a return by visiting our website and clicking on
'Returns'.\n"},
]

# Fine-tuning request (using OpenAI API)
response = openai.FineTune.create(
    training_file="file-id",  # Replace with your uploaded dataset
file ID
    model="text-davinci-003"
)
print("Fine-tuning job ID:", response["id"])
```

3. Deployment

- **Integration**:
  - Deployed the chatbot using a web API backed by Flask or FastAPI.
  - Integrated with the company's existing customer support platform.

- **Features**:
  - Escalation triggers for unhandled queries (e.g., "I need to speak to a human").
  - Personalization based on customer order history.

Code Example: Deploying the Chatbot

python

```python
from flask import Flask, request, jsonify
import openai

app = Flask(__name__)
openai.api_key = "your_openai_api_key"

@app.route("/support", methods=["POST"])
def support():
    user_query = request.json.get("query", "")
    response = openai.Completion.create(
        engine="text-davinci-003",
        prompt=f"Customer query: {user_query}\nResponse:",
        max_tokens=150,
        temperature=0.7,
    )
    reply = response.choices[0].text.strip()
    return jsonify({"reply": reply})

if __name__ == "__main__":
    app.run(host="0.0.0.0", port=5000)
```

Results

- **Query Resolution**: Automated responses resolved 70% of queries without human intervention.

- **Customer Satisfaction**: Reduced response time by 60%, improving customer experience.

- **Cost Savings**: Reduced workload allowed the support team to focus on high-priority issues, saving $200,000 annually.

Case Study 2: Fine-Tuning Models for Domain-Specific Applications

Problem Statement

A law firm required an AI system to summarize lengthy legal documents while retaining key details for faster client consultation. Generic LLMs failed to understand legal jargon accurately.

Solution

Fine-tuned a BERT model for legal document summarization, enabling precise extraction of key points.

Implementation Steps

1. Dataset Preparation

- **Source Data**:
    - Legal case files, contracts, and compliance reports.
- **Annotation**:
    - Domain experts annotated key points for each document, creating a parallel dataset for fine-tuning.

Dataset Example:

Document Text	Summary
"This agreement is entered into by..."	"Agreement between parties on terms X."
"The court finds the defendant guilty of..."	"Defendant convicted under section Y."

2. Fine-Tuning BERT for Summarization

- **Model Choice**:
    - Used legal-bert (a pretrained model for legal texts).
- **Framework**:
    - Hugging Face Transformers library.

Code Example:

python

```python
from transformers import AutoTokenizer, AutoModelForSeq2SeqLM,
Trainer, TrainingArguments
from datasets import load_dataset

# Load legal dataset
dataset = load_dataset("path/to/legal_dataset")

# Tokenizer and model
tokenizer = AutoTokenizer.from_pretrained("legal-bert")
model = AutoModelForSeq2SeqLM.from_pretrained("legal-bert")

# Preprocess data
def preprocess(data):
    inputs = tokenizer(data["text"], max_length=512, truncation=True,
padding="max_length")
    labels = tokenizer(data["summary"], max_length=150,
truncation=True, padding="max_length").input_ids
    inputs["labels"] = labels
    return inputs

tokenized_dataset = dataset.map(preprocess, batched=True)

# Fine-tune model
training_args = TrainingArguments(
    output_dir="./legal_model",
    evaluation_strategy="epoch",
    learning_rate=2e-5,
    per_device_train_batch_size=8,
    per_device_eval_batch_size=8,
    num_train_epochs=3,
    weight_decay=0.01,
)

trainer = Trainer(
    model=model,
    args=training_args,
    train_dataset=tokenized_dataset["train"],
    eval_dataset=tokenized_dataset["validation"],
)

trainer.train()
```

---

3. Deployment

- Integrated the fine-tuned model into the firm's document management system.

- Allowed lawyers to upload documents and receive summaries instantly.

Code Example: Deployment API

python

```python
from fastapi import FastAPI, Request
from transformers import AutoTokenizer, AutoModelForSeq2SeqLM

app = FastAPI()

# Load fine-tuned model
tokenizer = AutoTokenizer.from_pretrained("./legal_model")
model = AutoModelForSeq2SeqLM.from_pretrained("./legal_model")

@app.post("/summarize")
async def summarize(request: Request):
    data = await request.json()
    document = data.get("document", "")
    inputs = tokenizer(document, return_tensors="pt", max_length=512,
truncation=True)
    summary_ids = model.generate(inputs["input_ids"], max_length=150,
length_penalty=2.0, num_beams=4)
    summary = tokenizer.decode(summary_ids[0],
skip_special_tokens=True)
    return {"summary": summary}

if __name__ == "__main__":
    import uvicorn
    uvicorn.run(app, host="0.0.0.0", port=8000)
```

Results

- **Efficiency**: Reduced document review time by 40%.

- **Accuracy**: Achieved a 90% alignment rate with human-written summaries.

- **Scalability**: Processed up to 10,000 documents per month without performance degradation.

Summary

1. **Case Study 1**:

   o Automated customer support using GPT.

- Benefits included reduced response time, cost savings, and improved customer satisfaction.

2. **Case Study 2**:

- Fine-tuned a legal-focused LLM for document summarization.

- Enabled faster document processing and improved productivity in the legal domain.

3. **Key Takeaways**:

- Real-world applications demonstrate the transformative potential of LLMs across industries.

- Fine-tuning and integration are essential to tailor LLMs for specific domains.

This chapter provided practical insights into how LLMs solve real-world challenges. In the next chapter, we will explore techniques for maintaining and monitoring LLMs in production environments.

Chapter 7: Monitoring and Maintenance

Large Language Models (LLMs) deployed in production require continuous monitoring and maintenance to ensure consistent performance, detect anomalies, and adapt to changing conditions. This chapter focuses on setting up model observability, with tools and techniques to monitor model performance and detect drift.

7.1 Model Observability

Model observability refers to the ability to monitor and understand the behavior of a machine learning model in production. This involves tracking metrics like inference latency, accuracy, throughput, and detecting issues like data drift or performance degradation.

7.1.1 Tools for Monitoring Model Performance and Drift

Why Monitor Models in Production?

1. **Ensure Consistent Performance**:

   o Identify bottlenecks or performance drops during inference.

2. **Detect Data Drift**:

   o Data characteristics in production may differ from the training dataset, leading to degraded performance.

3. **Proactively Address Issues**:

   o Early detection of anomalies reduces downtime and improves user experience.

Key Metrics to Monitor

Metric	Description
Inference Latency	Time taken to process a single input
Throughput	Number of requests processed per second
Accuracy	Proportion of correct predictions
Data Drift	Changes in input data distribution over time
Model Drift	Deviation in model outputs due to data or environment changes

Tools for Monitoring

1. MLFlow

- **Purpose**: Track experiments, monitor metrics, and log models.
- **Features**:
  - Logging training and evaluation metrics.
  - Tracking deployment versions.
  - Comparing performance across multiple models.

2. Prometheus and Grafana

- **Purpose**: Real-time monitoring and visualization.
- **Features**:
  - Metrics collection with Prometheus.
  - Interactive dashboards with Grafana.

3. Seldon Core

- **Purpose**: Monitoring LLMs in Kubernetes-based environments.
- **Features**:
  - Built-in drift detection.
  - Explainability tools for model predictions.

Code: Set Up Monitoring and Logging with MLFlow

Objective

Log model inference metrics (e.g., latency and accuracy) and visualize them using MLFlow.

Prerequisites

1. Install MLFlow:

bash

```
pip install mlflow
```

2. Start the MLFlow tracking server:

bash

```
mlflow ui
Access the dashboard at http://127.0.0.1:5000.
```

Code Implementation

python

```python
import mlflow
import time
import random
from transformers import pipeline

# Initialize MLFlow
mlflow.set_tracking_uri("http://127.0.0.1:5000")
mlflow.set_experiment("LLM Monitoring")

# Load a pretrained model for inference
classifier = pipeline("sentiment-analysis")

# Simulate model inference and log metrics
with mlflow.start_run(run_name="Inference Monitoring"):
    for i in range(10):
        input_text = f"Sample input {i}"

        # Measure inference latency
        start_time = time.time()
        result = classifier(input_text)
        latency = time.time() - start_time

        # Simulate random accuracy for demonstration
        accuracy = random.uniform(0.8, 1.0)

        # Log metrics to MLFlow
        mlflow.log_metric("inference_latency", latency)
        mlflow.log_metric("accuracy", accuracy)

        print(f"Logged metrics for input {i}: Latency={latency:.4f}s,
Accuracy={accuracy:.2f}")
```

Explanation

1. **Experiment Setup**:

   o MLFlow tracks experiments and logs inference metrics (e.g., latency, accuracy).

2. **Simulated Inference**:

   o For demonstration, a sentiment analysis pipeline is used, and random accuracy is logged.

3. **Metrics Logging**:

   o mlflow.log_metric records metrics, which can be visualized in the MLFlow dashboard.

Exercise : Monitor Inference Performance in a Live Application

Objective: Set up real-time monitoring of inference performance (latency, throughput) for a deployed LLM using Prometheus and Grafana.

Steps:

1. Set Up Prometheus

1. **Install Prometheus**: Download and configure Prometheus from the official website.

2. **Configuration**: Update the Prometheus configuration (prometheus.yml) to scrape metrics from your application:

yaml

```
scrape_configs:
  - job_name: "llm_inference"
    static_configs:
      - targets: ["localhost:8000"]
```

2. Expose Metrics from the Application

Modify your FastAPI-based inference service to expose metrics using the prometheus_client library.

bash

```
pip install prometheus_client
```

Code Example:

python

```python
from fastapi import FastAPI, Request
from prometheus_client import Counter, Histogram, start_http_server

# Initialize FastAPI app
app = FastAPI()

# Define Prometheus metrics
INFERENCE_REQUESTS = Counter("inference_requests", "Number of
inference_requests")
INFERENCE_LATENCY = Histogram("inference_latency_seconds", "Latency of
inference_requests")

@app.get("/metrics")
async def metrics():
    from prometheus_client import generate_latest
    return generate_latest()

@app.post("/predict")
async def predict(request: Request):
    input_data = await request.json()
    text = input_data.get("text", "")

    INFERENCE_REQUESTS.inc()  # Increment request counter

    # Measure latency
    with INFERENCE_LATENCY.time():
        # Simulate inference
        result = {"text": text, "prediction": "positive"}

    return result

# Start Prometheus metrics server
if __name__ == "__main__":
    import uvicorn
    start_http_server(8001)  # Start metrics server
    uvicorn.run(app, host="0.0.0.0", port=8000)
```

3. Visualize Metrics with Grafana

1. **Install Grafana**: Download and configure Grafana from the official website.

2. **Connect Prometheus**: Add Prometheus as a data source in Grafana.

3. **Create Dashboards**: Use Prometheus queries to visualize metrics like:

   o inference_requests: Total inference requests.

   o rate(inference_latency_seconds[1m]): Average latency over the last minute.

Summary

1. **Model Observability**:

   o Tracking key metrics like inference latency, accuracy, and data drift ensures reliable performance in production.

2. **Tools for Monitoring**:

   o Tools like MLFlow, Prometheus, and Grafana provide robust capabilities for logging, monitoring, and visualizing metrics.

3. **Practical Implementations**:

   o MLFlow logging demonstrated how to track metrics during inference.

   o FastAPI and Prometheus integration showcased real-time monitoring for live applications.

By implementing these monitoring techniques, you can maintain robust and reliable LLM deployments. The next section will explore techniques for handling model updates and fine-tuning in dynamic environments.

7.2 Handling Model Updates

As data evolves and user requirements change, maintaining the relevance and performance of Large Language Models (LLMs) requires regular updates. This involves retraining or fine-tuning models on evolving datasets to adapt them to new information, reduce bias, and address emerging challenges.

7.2.1 Retraining and Fine-Tuning on Evolving Datasets

Why Update Models?

1. **Evolving Data**:

   o Data distributions change over time (e.g., user behavior, market trends).

- o Example: A news summarization model trained on 2020 data might miss nuances in 2024 topics.

2. **Improving Accuracy**:
   - o Incorporating new data improves model predictions.
   - o Example: A chatbot trained on new FAQs can better address recent customer concerns.

3. **Reducing Bias**:
   - o Retraining on diverse datasets can mitigate biases introduced during initial training.

Steps for Updating Models

---

1. Data Collection and Preprocessing

Collect New Data

- Sources:
  - o User interactions (e.g., chat logs, queries).
  - o Updated datasets (e.g., new legal texts, product catalogs).
  - o Feedback loops (e.g., flagged incorrect responses).

Example: For a sentiment analysis model:

- Collect recent social media posts, customer reviews, and survey responses.

Preprocess the Data

1. **Cleaning**:
   - o Remove irrelevant content (e.g., stop words, HTML tags).
   - o Handle missing or corrupted entries.

2. **Tokenization**:
   - o Convert text into tokens suitable for the LLM.
   - o Tools: Hugging Face Tokenizer, NLTK.

3. **Splitting**:

      o   Divide data into training, validation, and test sets.

Code Example: Preprocessing a Dataset for Fine-Tuning

python

```
from transformers import AutoTokenizer

# Load tokenizer
tokenizer = AutoTokenizer.from_pretrained("bert-base-uncased")

# Sample dataset
data = [
    "I love this product! It's amazing.",
    "The service was terrible and disappointing.",
]

# Tokenize data
tokenized_data = tokenizer(data, truncation=True, padding=True,
max_length=128, return_tensors="pt")

print(tokenized_data)
```

2. Fine-Tuning the Model

Model Selection

- **Transfer Learning**: Start with a pretrained model (e.g., GPT, BERT).
- Fine-tune on the new dataset for task-specific improvement.

Define the Objective

1. **Classification Tasks**:

   o   Example: Sentiment analysis.

   o   Objective: Minimize cross-entropy loss.

2. **Generation Tasks**:

   o   Example: Text summarization.

   o   Objective: Minimize sequence generation loss.

Code Example: Fine-Tuning BERT for Sentiment Analysis

Prerequisites:

- Install Hugging Face Transformers:

bash

```bash
pip install transformers datasets
```

Implementation:

python

```python
from transformers import AutoTokenizer,
AutoModelForSequenceClassification, Trainer, TrainingArguments
from datasets import load_dataset

# Load dataset
dataset = load_dataset("yelp_polarity")  # Example dataset

# Load tokenizer and model
model_name = "bert-base-uncased"
tokenizer = AutoTokenizer.from_pretrained(model_name)
model = AutoModelForSequenceClassification.from_pretrained(model_name,
num_labels=2)

# Preprocess data
def preprocess(data):
    return tokenizer(data["text"], truncation=True, padding=True,
max_length=128)

tokenized_dataset = dataset.map(preprocess, batched=True)

# Define training arguments
training_args = TrainingArguments(
    output_dir="./results",
    evaluation_strategy="epoch",
    learning_rate=2e-5,
    per_device_train_batch_size=16,
    num_train_epochs=3,
    weight_decay=0.01,
)

# Initialize Trainer
trainer = Trainer(
    model=model,
```

```
    args=training_args,
    train_dataset=tokenized_dataset["train"],
    eval_dataset=tokenized_dataset["test"],
    tokenizer=tokenizer,
)

# Fine-tune the model
trainer.train()
```

3. Testing and Validation

Evaluate Model Performance

- Metrics:

    - **Accuracy**: Percentage of correct predictions.

    - **F1-Score**: Balances precision and recall.

    - **BLEU/ROUGE**: For text generation tasks.

Example: Evaluate Accuracy

python

```
from sklearn.metrics import accuracy_score

# Predictions and labels
predictions = [0, 1, 0, 1]  # Example model outputs
labels = [0, 1, 1, 1]  # Ground truth

# Calculate accuracy
accuracy = accuracy_score(labels, predictions)
print(f"Accuracy: {accuracy * 100:.2f}%")
```

4. Deployment

Version Control

- Save the updated model with version tagging.

- Example: v1.1 for a newly fine-tuned model.

A/B Testing

- Deploy the updated model alongside the original.

- Compare performance metrics to validate improvement.

Gradual Rollout

- Roll out updates to a subset of users first.
- Monitor performance and adjust before full deployment.

Code Example: Saving and Loading Models

python

```python
from transformers import AutoModelForSequenceClassification

# Save model
model.save_pretrained("./fine_tuned_model")

# Load model
model = AutoModelForSequenceClassification.from_pretrained("./fine_tuned_model")
```

Challenges and Solutions

Challenge	Solution
Data Drift	Regularly collect and annotate production data.
Resource Constraints	Use mixed-precision training or cloud-based GPUs.
Deployment Downtime	Use canary or blue-green deployments to avoid interruptions.
Bias in New Data	Perform bias audits and ensure balanced representation in retraining data.

Exercise: Retrain a Model on Evolving Sentiment Data

Objective: Fine-tune a sentiment analysis model using recent social media posts.

Steps:

1. Collect social media data from a specific platform (e.g., Twitter).
2. Preprocess the data for classification tasks.
3. Fine-tune a pretrained BERT model.
4. Test and validate the updated model.

Outcome:

- Improved accuracy on real-time sentiment predictions.

Summary

1. **Why Model Updates Are Necessary**:

   o Data evolves over time, requiring retraining or fine-tuning to maintain performance.

2. **Steps for Updating Models**:

   o Data collection, preprocessing, fine-tuning, validation, and deployment.

   o Example code demonstrated the process for a sentiment analysis model.

3. **Best Practices**:

   o Regularly monitor performance metrics.

   o Use A/B testing and version control for seamless updates.

By mastering model updates, you can ensure that your LLMs remain relevant and effective in dynamic environments. In the next section, we will explore strategies for ensuring fairness, ethics, and compliance in LLM deployment.

7.3 Ethics and Compliance

Ethical considerations and compliance standards are essential when deploying Large Language Models (LLMs). This section addresses strategies for ensuring fairness, reducing bias, and meeting data privacy standards to ensure responsible AI deployment.

7.3.1 Ensuring Fairness, Reducing Bias, and Meeting Data Privacy Standards

Why Ethics and Compliance Matter

1. **Fairness**:

   o LLMs must provide equitable outputs for diverse user groups.

   o Biases in models can perpetuate stereotypes or discriminatory practices.

2. **Bias Reduction**:

   o Training datasets may reflect historical or societal biases, which the model can inadvertently learn and propagate.

3. **Data Privacy**:

o   Compliance with regulations like GDPR (General Data Protection Regulation) and CCPA (California Consumer Privacy Act) is mandatory when handling sensitive user data.

4. **Trust and Accountability**:

o   Ensuring ethical practices builds trust among users and stakeholders.

Strategies for Ensuring Fairness

1. Dataset Diversity

- **Problem**: Homogeneous datasets lead to biased outputs.

- **Solution**:

o   Use diverse and representative datasets covering different demographics, languages, and cultures.

o   Balance datasets to avoid over-representation or under-representation of any group.

Example: If building a sentiment analysis model:

- Include reviews from various regions, age groups, and socio-economic backgrounds.

---

2. Bias Audits

- **Definition**: Evaluate the model's outputs for potential biases during development and deployment.

- **Implementation**:

o   Use **test cases** designed to detect biases.

o   Example: Check if the model favors specific gender pronouns or makes biased assumptions.

Code Example: Simple Bias Detection Test

python

```python
from transformers import pipeline

# Load sentiment analysis pipeline
model = pipeline("sentiment-analysis", model="distilbert-base-uncased")
```

```
# Test phrases
phrases = [
    "She is a nurse.",
    "He is a doctor.",
    "They are great leaders.",
]

# Analyze biases in outputs
results = {phrase: model(phrase) for phrase in phrases}
for phrase, result in results.items():
    print(f"Phrase: {phrase}, Sentiment: {result}")
```

---

3. Post-Processing

- Adjust outputs to ensure equitable representation.

- Example: Normalize probabilities for sensitive attributes (e.g., gender, race).

Reducing Bias

1. Bias Mitigation During Training

- **Techniques**:

    - **Adversarial Training**:

        - Introduce adversarial examples during training to improve robustness.

    - **Debiasing Algorithms**:

        - Use methods like **Equalized Odds Postprocessing** to adjust predictions.

- **Tools**:

    - IBM AI Fairness 360 (AIF360): A library for detecting and mitigating bias.

Code Example: Using AIF360 for Bias Detection

python

```
from aif360.datasets import AdultDataset
from aif360.metrics import BinaryLabelDatasetMetric

# Load dataset
dataset = AdultDataset()
```

```
# Check for bias
metric = BinaryLabelDatasetMetric(dataset,
unprivileged_groups=[{'sex': 0}], privileged_groups=[{'sex': 1}])
print("Disparate Impact:", metric.disparate_impact())
```

2. Model Interpretability

- Explainability tools help identify why models make certain predictions.
- **SHAP (SHapley Additive exPlanations)**:
  - Explains individual predictions by attributing them to input features.

Code Example: Using SHAP for Explainability

python

```
import shap
from transformers import AutoModelForSequenceClassification,
AutoTokenizer

# Load model and tokenizer
model_name = "distilbert-base-uncased"
model = AutoModelForSequenceClassification.from_pretrained(model_name)
tokenizer = AutoTokenizer.from_pretrained(model_name)

# Create SHAP explainer
explainer = shap.Explainer(model, tokenizer)

# Test input
inputs = tokenizer("This is a great product!", return_tensors="pt")
shap_values = explainer(inputs["input_ids"])
shap.plots.text(shap_values)
```

Meeting Data Privacy Standards

1. Compliance with Regulations

- **GDPR** (Europe):
  - Ensure user consent for data collection and processing.
  - Provide users with the right to access, modify, or delete their data.
- **CCPA** (California):
  - Allow users to opt out of data sales.

       o Implement robust data security measures.

2. Anonymization and Encryption

- **Anonymization**:
  - o Remove personally identifiable information (PII) from datasets.
  - o Example: Replace names with generic tokens (e.g., [NAME]).

- **Encryption**:
  - o Encrypt sensitive data both in transit and at rest.

Code Example: Data Anonymization with Python

python

```
import re

# Example dataset
data = [
    "John Doe bought a car.",
    "Jane Smith visited the store.",
]

# Anonymize names
anonymized_data = [re.sub(r"\b[A-Z][a-z]+\s[A-Z][a-z]+\b", "[NAME]",
text) for text in data]
print(anonymized_data)
```

---

3. Differential Privacy

- Introduce noise to datasets or model outputs to prevent identification of individual data points.
- Example: Apply **TensorFlow Privacy** during model training.

Code Example: Using TensorFlow Privacy

python

```
import tensorflow as tf
from tensorflow_privacy import DPAdamGaussianOptimizer

# Define model and optimizer
model = tf.keras.Sequential([
    tf.keras.layers.Dense(10, activation='relu', input_shape=(20,)),
```

```
    tf.keras.layers.Dense(1, activation='sigmoid')
])

optimizer = DPAdamGaussianOptimizer(
    l2_norm_clip=1.0,
    noise_multiplier=0.5,
    num_microbatches=1,
    learning_rate=0.01
)

model.compile(optimizer=optimizer, loss='binary_crossentropy',
metrics=['accuracy'])
```

Summary

1. **Ensuring Fairness**:

    o Use diverse datasets, conduct bias audits, and post-process outputs to ensure equitable performance.

2. **Reducing Bias**:

    o Implement adversarial training, debiasing algorithms, and model interpretability techniques.

3. **Meeting Data Privacy Standards**:

    o Ensure compliance with regulations like GDPR and CCPA.

    o Apply anonymization, encryption, and differential privacy to safeguard user data.

4. **Practical Tools**:

    o Libraries like AIF360 and SHAP provide robust frameworks for fairness and explainability.

    o TensorFlow Privacy enables privacy-preserving model training.

By addressing these ethical and compliance challenges, you can ensure responsible AI deployment while maintaining user trust and adhering to legal standards. The next chapter will summarize key takeaways and provide a forward-looking perspective on the evolution of LLM engineering.

Chapter 8: Emerging Trends and Future Directions

Learning Objectives

By the end of this chapter, you will:

1. Understand the advancements in multimodal models that combine text, images, and audio.

2. Explore real-world applications that leverage multimodal capabilities for richer AI experiences.

3. Learn about the tools and frameworks enabling the development of multimodal AI systems.

8.1 Advances in Multimodal Models

Multimodal models represent a significant leap in AI, enabling systems to process and generate outputs across multiple modalities, such as text, images, and audio. These models open the door to more interactive and enriched AI applications.

8.1.1 Combining Text, Images, and Audio for Richer AI Applications

What are Multimodal Models?

- **Definition**: Multimodal models integrate data from multiple sources (text, images, audio) to perform tasks that require understanding and generating content across these modalities.

- **Examples**:
  - **Text-to-Image**: Generating images from textual descriptions.
  - **Visual Question Answering (VQA)**: Answering questions based on images.
  - **Speech-to-Text and Beyond**: Combining speech transcription with contextual understanding for more intelligent virtual assistants.

Key Components of Multimodal Models

1. **Encoders for Each Modality**:
   - Text: Tokenization and embedding layers for textual data.

- Images: Convolutional or Vision Transformer (ViT) models.
- Audio: Spectrogram-based processing or waveform encoders.

2. **Cross-Modality Attention**:
   - Mechanism that learns relationships between different modalities.
   - Example: Attention linking words in a caption to objects in an image.

3. **Unified Representations**:
   - Embedding spaces that unify features from all modalities for consistent understanding.

Applications of Multimodal Models

1. **Text-to-Image Generation**:
   - **Example**: DALL-E generates creative art based on textual prompts.

2. **Visual Question Answering (VQA)**:
   - **Example**: Answering "What color is the cat?" when provided with an image of a cat.

3. **Interactive Virtual Assistants**:
   - **Example**: Alexa or Google Assistant processing both voice commands and visual inputs like images.

4. **Video Analysis**:
   - Integrating speech, subtitles, and visual frames for comprehensive analysis.

Code Example: Text-to-Image Generation Using DALL-E

Objective: Generate an image based on a textual description.

Prerequisites:

1. Install OpenAI API:

bash

```
pip install openai
```
Implementation:

python

```python
import openai

# OpenAI API Key
openai.api_key = "your_openai_api_key"

# Function to generate image
def generate_image(prompt):
    response = openai.Image.create(
        prompt=prompt,
        n=1,
        size="512x512"
    )
    return response['data'][0]['url']

# Example usage
prompt = "A futuristic cityscape at sunset with flying cars"
image_url = generate_image(prompt)
print(f"Generated Image URL: {image_url}")
```

Code Example: Visual Question Answering with BLIP

Objective: Answer questions about an image.

Prerequisites:

1. Install Hugging Face Transformers:

bash

```bash
pip install transformers
```

Implementation:

python

```python
from transformers import BlipProcessor, BlipForQuestionAnswering
from PIL import Image

# Load model and processor
processor = BlipProcessor.from_pretrained("Salesforce/blip-vqa-base")
model = BlipForQuestionAnswering.from_pretrained("Salesforce/blip-vqa-base")
```

```
# Load an image
image = Image.open("example_image.jpg")

# Prepare inputs
question = "What is in the image?"
inputs = processor(image, question, return_tensors="pt")

# Generate answer
outputs = model.generate(**inputs)
answer = processor.decode(outputs[0], skip_special_tokens=True)
print(f"Answer: {answer}")
```

Explanation:

- **Input**: An image and a related question.

- **Output**: A text-based answer derived by analyzing the visual and textual data.

Frameworks for Building Multimodal Models

Framework	Description
Hugging Face Transformers	Pretrained models for multimodal tasks like VQA and text-to-image generation.
OpenAI API	Supports advanced models like DALL-E for text-to-image capabilities.
PyTorch Lightning	Simplifies multimodal model training and evaluation.
TensorFlow	Offers tools for integrating multiple data modalities.

Challenges in Multimodal AI

Challenge	Solution
Data Alignment	Use paired datasets (e.g., image-caption datasets) for training.
Computational Costs	Optimize using model compression techniques (e.g., quantization, pruning).
Interpretability	Employ explainability tools like SHAP for multimodal outputs.
Limited Resources	Leverage pretrained models like CLIP, BLIP, and DALL-E.

Future Directions in Multimodal AI

1. **Real-Time Multimodal Applications**:

   o Seamless integration of video, audio, and text for immersive experiences.

   o Example: Real-time translation combining speech and visual cues.

2. **Personalized Multimodal AI**:

   o Models that adapt based on user preferences across multiple modalities.

   o Example: Personalized video summaries combining audio cues and text overlays.

3. **Edge Deployment**:

   o Deploying multimodal models on edge devices for low-latency applications.

Summary

1. **Advancements in Multimodal Models**:

   o Multimodal models like DALL-E and BLIP enable integration across text, image, and audio data.

2. **Applications**:

   o Text-to-image generation, visual question answering, and interactive virtual assistants illustrate the potential of multimodal AI.

3. **Hands-On Practice**:

   o Practical code examples demonstrated building multimodal applications with popular frameworks.

4. **Challenges and Solutions**:

   o Addressing data alignment and computational costs ensures effective multimodal AI implementation.

This chapter explored the cutting-edge advancements in multimodal AI, setting the stage for transformative applications in the future. In the next section, we will discuss smaller, efficient LLMs and their implications for real-world use cases.

8.2 Smaller, More Efficient Models

As Large Language Models (LLMs) grow increasingly complex, the demand for smaller, more efficient models capable of achieving similar performance has risen. This section explores emerging techniques like **LoRA (Low-Rank Adaptation)** and other strategies to create compact, resource-efficient models for real-world applications.

8.2.1 LoRA (Low-Rank Adaptation) and Other Emerging Techniques

What is LoRA (Low-Rank Adaptation)?

LoRA is a technique for fine-tuning large language models efficiently. Instead of updating all the parameters of a model during fine-tuning, LoRA introduces low-rank matrices to adapt the pretrained model. This significantly reduces the computational and storage requirements.

How LoRA Works

1. **Pretrained Model**:

   o   Start with a pretrained model (e.g., GPT, BERT).

2. **Low-Rank Matrices**:

   o   Introduce low-rank matrices (A and B) to approximate parameter updates instead of updating the full weight matrix.

Mathematical Representation: If W is the weight matrix of the model, LoRA modifies it as:

$$W' = W + A \cdot B W' = W + A \cdot B W' = W + A \cdot B$$

where:

   o   A and B are low-rank matrices.

   o   W' is the adapted weight matrix.

3. **Efficiency**:

   o   Only the small A and B matrices are trained, reducing memory and computation.

Advantages of LoRA

Aspect	Benefit
Efficiency	Reduces fine-tuning costs by training a small fraction of parameters.
Modularity	Multiple tasks can have their own low-rank adaptations without modifying the base model.
Compatibility	Compatible with large-scale models like GPT and T5.

Code Example: Fine-Tuning with LoRA

Objective: Fine-tune a GPT model using LoRA for a sentiment analysis task.

Prerequisites:

1. Install Hugging Face Transformers and LoRA library:

bash

```
pip install transformers peft
```

Implementation:

python

```python
from transformers import AutoModelForCausalLM, AutoTokenizer
from peft import get_peft_model, LoraConfig, TaskType

# Load pretrained model and tokenizer
model_name = "gpt2"
model = AutoModelForCausalLM.from_pretrained(model_name)
tokenizer = AutoTokenizer.from_pretrained(model_name)

# Define LoRA configuration
config = LoraConfig(
    task_type=TaskType.CAUSAL_LM,  # Type of task (e.g., causal
language modeling)
    inference_mode=False,
    r=8,  # Rank of the low-rank matrices
    lora_alpha=16,  # Scaling factor
    lora_dropout=0.1  # Dropout for regularization
)

# Apply LoRA to the model
lora_model = get_peft_model(model, config)

# Example fine-tuning data
text = "The product was fantastic!"
inputs = tokenizer(text, return_tensors="pt")
outputs = lora_model(**inputs, labels=inputs["input_ids"])

# Compute loss and optimize (for demonstration purposes)
loss = outputs.loss
loss.backward()
print(f"Loss: {loss.item()}")
```

Other Emerging Techniques

1. Knowledge Distillation

- Train a smaller **student model** to mimic the behavior of a larger **teacher model**.

- **Advantages**:
    - Reduces model size.
    - Maintains high performance on specific tasks.

Example: Distill GPT-3 into a smaller GPT-2-like model for faster inference.

Code Example:

python

```python
from transformers import AutoModelForSequenceClassification, Trainer,
TrainingArguments

# Load teacher and student models
teacher_model =
AutoModelForSequenceClassification.from_pretrained("bert-large-
uncased")
student_model =
AutoModelForSequenceClassification.from_pretrained("bert-small-
uncased")

# Define training arguments
training_args = TrainingArguments(
    output_dir="./distilled_model",
    learning_rate=3e-5,
    num_train_epochs=3,
    per_device_train_batch_size=16,
)

# Set up trainer
trainer = Trainer(
    model=student_model,
    args=training_args,
    train_dataset=train_dataset,
    teacher_model=teacher_model,  # Use teacher for distillation
)

trainer.train()
```

2. Quantization

- o Reduce model size by lowering the precision of parameters (e.g., from 32-bit floating-point to 8-bit integers).

- o **Benefits**:

  - • Faster inference.

  - • Lower memory requirements.

Code Example: Quantizing a Model with PyTorch

python

```
import torch
from transformers import AutoModelForSequenceClassification

# Load model
model = AutoModelForSequenceClassification.from_pretrained("bert-base-
uncased")

# Apply dynamic quantization
quantized_model = torch.quantization.quantize_dynamic(
    model, {torch.nn.Linear}, dtype=torch.qint8
)

print("Quantized model:", quantized_model)
```

3. Pruning

- o Remove insignificant weights or neurons to simplify the model.

- o **Structured Pruning**:

  - • Remove entire layers or filters.

- o **Unstructured Pruning**:

  - • Remove individual weights close to zero.

Example: PyTorch Pruning

python

```
import torch.nn.utils.prune as prune
```

```
# Apply pruning to a model layer
prune.random_unstructured(model.classifier, name="weight", amount=0.3)
print("Pruned model:", model.classifier)
```

4. **Sparse Models**

   o Replace dense layers with sparse matrices to reduce computation.

   o **Example**: Mixture of Experts (MoE) models activate only a subset of experts for each input.

Comparison of Techniques

Technique	Reduction in Size	Inference Speed	Performance
LoRA	Moderate	High	Maintains task-specific performance.
Knowledge Distillation	High	High	Slight drop in accuracy.
Quantization	High	Very High	May lose precision in outputs.
Pruning	Moderate	Moderate	May lose some accuracy.

Challenges in Creating Smaller Models

Challenge	Solution
Performance Drop	Use advanced fine-tuning techniques like LoRA or knowledge distillation.
Hardware Compatibility	Ensure quantized models are supported on target hardware (e.g., GPUs, TPUs).
Limited Generalization	Fine-tune smaller models on diverse datasets to improve robustness.

Summary

1. **LoRA (Low-Rank Adaptation):**

153

- Efficiently fine-tunes models by introducing low-rank matrices, reducing computational costs.

2. **Emerging Techniques**:

  - Knowledge distillation, quantization, pruning, and sparse modeling offer diverse methods to create smaller, faster models.

3. **Hands-On Practice**:

  - Code examples demonstrated practical implementation of LoRA and other optimization techniques.

4. **Impact**:

  - These techniques make LLMs accessible for resource-constrained environments while maintaining performance.

By adopting these methods, organizations can leverage the power of LLMs in cost-effective and scalable ways, paving the way for broader adoption across industries.

8.3 Challenges and Opportunities Ahead

As Large Language Models (LLMs) continue to evolve, they present both significant challenges and exciting opportunities. This section explores the **environmental costs** of training LLMs and the growing focus on **personalization**, discussing how these factors will shape the future of LLM engineering.

8.3.1 Environmental Costs of LLM Training

The Challenge: Energy Consumption

Training LLMs requires substantial computational resources, leading to significant energy consumption and carbon emissions. For example:

- Training **GPT-3** consumed **1,287 MWh of electricity**, emitting approximately **552 tons of CO_2**—comparable to the yearly emissions of 60 average U.S. homes.

Sources of Energy Consumption

1. **Model Training**:

  - Requires multiple GPUs or TPUs running continuously for weeks or months.

  - Example: Training a single large LLM may involve **millions of GPU hours**.

2. **Inference**:

o   Large-scale deployments with millions of daily users amplify energy usage during inference.

Strategies to Mitigate Environmental Costs

1. Optimize Model Architectures

- Use efficient architectures like **sparse models** (e.g., Mixture of Experts) to reduce unnecessary computations.

- Example: Activate only relevant parts of the model for each query.

2. Use Green Energy Sources

- Deploy data centers powered by renewable energy (e.g., solar, wind).

- Example: Google Cloud and AWS have initiatives for carbon-neutral infrastructure.

3. Quantization and Pruning

- Apply techniques like **quantization** and **pruning** to reduce the size and complexity of models, thus lowering energy requirements.

Code Example: Quantization for Efficient Inference

python

```
import torch
from transformers import AutoModelForSequenceClassification

# Load model
model = AutoModelForSequenceClassification.from_pretrained("bert-base-
uncased")

# Apply dynamic quantization
quantized_model = torch.quantization.quantize_dynamic(
    model, {torch.nn.Linear}, dtype=torch.qint8
)
print("Quantized model:", quantized_model)
```

4. Distributed Training and Efficiency

- Leverage distributed training with advanced techniques like **gradient checkpointing** and **mixed precision** to reduce resource usage.

Code Example: Mixed Precision Training with PyTorch

python

```
from torch.cuda.amp import GradScaler, autocast

scaler = GradScaler()

for epoch in range(epochs):
    for inputs, labels in dataloader:
        optimizer.zero_grad()
        with autocast():  # Use mixed precision
            outputs = model(inputs)
            loss = criterion(outputs, labels)
        scaler.scale(loss).backward()
        scaler.step(optimizer)
        scaler.update()
```

5. Embrace Pretraining and Fine-Tuning

- Pretrain a general-purpose model once and fine-tune it for specific tasks, avoiding redundant computations.

6. Monitor and Optimize Data Usage

- Ensure training data is curated efficiently to avoid unnecessary processing of irrelevant or redundant samples.

8.3.2 Personalization and the Future of LLMs

The Opportunity: Personalization

Personalization in LLMs involves tailoring models to individual users or specific contexts. This improves user engagement, relevance, and accuracy.

Benefits of Personalization

1. **User-Specific Responses**:
   - Example: A personalized chatbot could remember a user's preferences, such as favorite genres in book recommendations.

2. **Domain Adaptation**:
   - Models can specialize in niche fields (e.g., medical or legal advice).

3. **Improved Accuracy**:

o   Personalization enables models to fine-tune outputs based on historical data or specific user needs.

Techniques for Personalization

1. Fine-Tuning on User Data

- Fine-tune a general LLM on a small dataset specific to a user or domain.

Example: Fine-Tuning for Personalized Recommendations

python

```
from transformers import Trainer, TrainingArguments,
AutoModelForSequenceClassification, AutoTokenizer

# Load pretrained model and tokenizer
model =
AutoModelForSequenceClassification.from_pretrained("distilbert-base-
uncased")
tokenizer = AutoTokenizer.from_pretrained("distilbert-base-uncased")

# Fine-tune with user-specific data
train_dataset = ...   # Your user-specific dataset
training_args = TrainingArguments(
    output_dir="./personalized_model",
    per_device_train_batch_size=16,
    num_train_epochs=3,
    learning_rate=2e-5,
)
trainer = Trainer(
    model=model,
    args=training_args,
    train_dataset=train_dataset,
)
trainer.train()
```

2. Contextual Embeddings

- Use context-specific embeddings that adapt to the user's current input.
- Example: In a customer support scenario, embeddings could prioritize resolving past issues logged by the user.

3. Federated Learning

- Train models on user devices without uploading data to centralized servers, preserving privacy while improving personalization.

- Example: Google's **Gboard** keyboard uses federated learning for personalized suggestions.

Challenges in Personalization

Challenge	Solution
Data Privacy	Employ techniques like federated learning and differential privacy.
Scalability	Optimize fine-tuning to scale personalization across millions of users.
Bias Amplification	Use diverse and unbiased datasets to avoid reinforcing user-specific biases.

The Future of LLMs

1. **Smaller, Decentralized Models**:

   o Efficient LLMs deployed on edge devices, enabling real-time, low-latency personalization.

2. **Multimodal Personalization**:

   o Integration of text, images, and audio for richer, context-aware user interactions.

3. **Proactive AI**:

   o Predict user needs before explicit queries, based on behavioral patterns.

Summary

1. **Environmental Costs of LLMs**:

   o High energy consumption and carbon emissions pose a challenge.

   o Solutions like quantization, distributed training, and green energy adoption can mitigate these issues.

2. **Personalization**:

- o Tailored LLMs improve user engagement and domain-specific performance.
- o Techniques like fine-tuning, contextual embeddings, and federated learning enable efficient personalization.

3. **Opportunities**:

- o Advances in personalization and efficiency will drive the next generation of LLMs.
- o The future will see smaller, multimodal, and proactive AI systems.

By addressing these challenges and leveraging opportunities, the field of LLM engineering is poised to revolutionize AI applications across industries. The final chapter will summarize the key takeaways and provide actionable steps for readers to contribute to this exciting field.

Conclusion

This book has journeyed through the fascinating and complex world of Large Language Models (LLMs), exploring their inner workings, applications, and future potential. In this conclusion, we will recap the key takeaways and outline actionable steps to effectively apply LLMs in real-world projects.

Recap of Key Takeaways

1. Foundations of LLMs

- **Understanding the Basics**:
    - LLMs like GPT, BERT, and T5 rely on the Transformer architecture, leveraging self-attention and positional encoding for superior natural language understanding and generation.

- **Core Components**:
    - Tokenization, embeddings, multi-head attention, and feedforward networks form the building blocks of LLMs.

- **Popular Models**:
    - OpenAI's GPT excels at text generation.
    - BERT and its variants shine in tasks like sentiment analysis and question answering.
    - T5 is ideal for text-to-text tasks such as summarization and translation.

---

2. Designing and Training LLMs

- **Dataset Preparation**:
    - Clean, diverse, and domain-specific datasets are critical for high-performing models.

- **Training Techniques**:
    - Fine-tuning pretrained models on task-specific data is more efficient than training from scratch.
    - Techniques like LoRA (Low-Rank Adaptation), mixed precision training, and distributed training optimize resource usage.

- **Model Optimization**:

o   Quantization, pruning, and knowledge distillation enable efficient inference on resource-constrained devices.

3. Deploying LLMs

- **Inference Pipelines**:

    o   Tools like FastAPI, Flask, and Docker simplify the deployment of LLM-based APIs.

- **Scalability**:

    o   Elastic scaling using Kubernetes and cloud-native solutions ensures reliability during traffic spikes.

- **Security**:

    o   Protecting APIs from abuse and ensuring ethical use are essential in deployment.

4. Real-World Applications

- **Industry-Specific Use Cases**:

    o   Customer support chatbots, content generation, summarization, and sentiment analysis demonstrate the versatility of LLMs.

- **Multimodal AI**:

    o   Combining text, images, and audio enables richer applications like visual question answering and interactive virtual assistants.

5. Monitoring, Maintenance, and Ethics

- **Model Observability**:

    o   Tools like MLFlow and Prometheus facilitate monitoring inference performance and detecting model drift.

- **Updates and Fine-Tuning**:

    o   Regular retraining on evolving datasets ensures relevance and accuracy.

- **Ethics and Compliance**:

    o   Addressing bias, ensuring fairness, and complying with privacy standards are non-negotiable for responsible AI deployment.

6. Emerging Trends

- **Efficient Models**:
    - Techniques like LoRA and sparse modeling make LLMs accessible and scalable for diverse use cases.
- **Future Directions**:
    - Smaller, personalized, and environmentally conscious LLMs will redefine the AI landscape.

Actionable Steps for Applying LLMs in Real-World Projects

Step 1: Define Your Objectives

- Identify the problem you want to solve and how an LLM can address it.
- Example Objectives:
    - Automate customer support.
    - Generate high-quality marketing content.
    - Analyze customer sentiment from social media data.

Step 2: Choose the Right Model

- **General-Purpose Tasks**:
    - Use pretrained models like GPT for text generation or BERT for classification.
- **Domain-Specific Applications**:
    - Fine-tune models on task-specific datasets.
    - Example: Fine-tune BERT for legal document summarization.

Step 3: Prepare Your Dataset

- Collect and preprocess data to ensure it aligns with your objectives.
- Example:
    - For sentiment analysis:

- Source data from reviews or social media.
- Label the data (e.g., positive, neutral, negative).

Step 4: Optimize and Train

- Fine-tune pretrained models instead of training from scratch to save resources.
- Use optimization techniques like:
  - **Mixed Precision Training** for faster computations.
  - **Quantization** for reduced inference latency.

Code Example: Fine-Tuning GPT

python

```python
from transformers import AutoTokenizer, AutoModelForCausalLM, Trainer,
TrainingArguments

# Load pretrained model and tokenizer
tokenizer = AutoTokenizer.from_pretrained("gpt2")
model = AutoModelForCausalLM.from_pretrained("gpt2")

# Fine-tune with task-specific data
train_dataset = ...   # Your dataset here
training_args = TrainingArguments(
    output_dir="./results",
    per_device_train_batch_size=8,
    num_train_epochs=3,
    learning_rate=5e-5,
)
trainer = Trainer(
    model=model,
    args=training_args,
    train_dataset=train_dataset,
)
trainer.train()
```

Step 5: Deploy the Model

- Choose deployment strategies based on your requirements:
  - **APIs**: Use FastAPI or Flask to serve the model.

- Cloud Deployment: Leverage AWS, Azure, or Google Cloud for scalability.
- On-Premises: For privacy-sensitive applications, deploy the model locally.

Example: Deploying with FastAPI

python

```
from fastapi import FastAPI
from transformers import AutoModelForSequenceClassification,
AutoTokenizer

app = FastAPI()

# Load model and tokenizer
model =
AutoModelForSequenceClassification.from_pretrained("./model_dir")
tokenizer = AutoTokenizer.from_pretrained("bert-base-uncased")

@app.post("/predict")
async def predict(input_text: str):
    inputs = tokenizer(input_text, return_tensors="pt")
    outputs = model(**inputs)
    prediction = outputs.logits.argmax(dim=-1).item()
    return {"prediction": prediction}

if __name__ == "__main__":
    import uvicorn
    uvicorn.run(app, host="0.0.0.0", port=8000)
```

Step 6: Monitor and Maintain

- Use tools like **MLFlow** for tracking metrics.
- Monitor inference latency, throughput, and data drift using **Prometheus** and **Grafana**.
- Regularly update the model to adapt to new data and improve performance.

Step 7: Address Ethical and Compliance Considerations

- Conduct bias audits and ensure datasets are representative.
- Comply with data privacy laws like GDPR and CCPA.

- Use explainability tools like **SHAP** for transparent decision-making.

Step 8: Stay Updated

- Follow advancements in LLM research, including:
    - Multimodal models.
    - Techniques for smaller and more efficient LLMs.
    - Emerging tools for personalization and privacy.

Final Thoughts

The field of LLM engineering is rapidly evolving, offering immense potential to transform industries and improve lives. By understanding the foundational principles, leveraging advanced techniques, and addressing ethical considerations, you can harness the full power of LLMs to drive innovation and solve real-world challenges.

With the actionable steps outlined here, you are equipped to confidently apply LLMs in your projects and stay ahead in the dynamic world of AI.

Appendices

The appendices provide supplemental information to enhance your understanding of Large Language Models (LLMs) and serve as a practical reference for further exploration. This section includes a glossary of key terms, references for recommended reading, and access to a GitHub repository containing all sample code, datasets, and exercises from this book.

---

1. Glossary of Key Terms

This glossary defines essential terms and concepts used throughout the book, ensuring clarity for readers at all levels.

Term	Definition
Attention Mechanism	A method enabling models to focus on relevant parts of the input for better predictions.
BERT	Bidirectional Encoder Representations from Transformers; a model designed for tasks like classification and question answering.
Causal Language Modeling	Predicting the next token in a sequence, used in autoregressive models like GPT.
Data Drift	Changes in the data distribution over time, leading to potential model performance degradation.
Embedding	Dense vector representations of text or tokens, capturing semantic meaning.
Fine-Tuning	Adapting a pretrained model to a specific task using task-specific data.
Gradient Descent	An optimization algorithm to minimize the loss function during training.
Inference	The process of using a trained model to make predictions on new data.
LoRA (Low-Rank Adaptation)	A technique for efficient fine-tuning using low-rank matrices.
Multimodal Models	AI systems that integrate and process multiple data types, such as text, images, and audio.
Quantization	Reducing the precision of model parameters to improve

Term	Definition
	efficiency.
Self-Attention	A mechanism that helps models weigh the importance of different parts of the input.
Transfer Learning	Leveraging knowledge from a pretrained model for a new, related task.
Transformer	A deep learning architecture that uses self-attention for natural language processing tasks.

2. References and Recommended Reading

Core Reading

1. **Attention Is All You Need**

    o Vaswani et al., 2017.

    o The foundational paper introducing the Transformer architecture.

2. **BERT: Pre-training of Deep Bidirectional Transformers for Language Understanding**

    o Devlin et al., 2018.

    o A detailed look into BERT and its applications.

3. **Language Models Are Few-Shot Learners**

    o Brown et al., 2020.

    o The paper behind GPT-3, discussing its architecture and zero-shot capabilities.

Books

1. **Deep Learning for Natural Language Processing**

    o Palash Goyal, Sumit Pandey, Karan Jain.

    o A practical guide to NLP techniques and implementations.

2. **Natural Language Processing with Transformers**

    o Lewis Tunstall, Leandro von Werra, Thomas Wolf.

    o Covers applications of Hugging Face Transformers in NLP tasks.

3. **Designing Machine Learning Systems**

    o Chip Huyen.

    o Focused on designing scalable and efficient ML systems, including LLMs.

Online Courses and Tutorials

1. **CS224N: Natural Language Processing with Deep Learning**

    o Stanford University.

    o Available on YouTube and Stanford's website.

2. **Hugging Face Transformers Documentation**

    o Comprehensive documentation on the Transformers library.

    o Documentation Link

3. **FastAI's Practical Deep Learning for Coders**

    o Free course introducing deep learning concepts.

Research Blogs

1. **OpenAI Blog**

    o Latest research and insights on GPT models and other AI advancements.

2. **The Gradient**

    o A platform for discussing cutting-edge AI research and applications.

3. **Distill.pub**

    o Interactive, visually-rich explanations of deep learning concepts.

3. GitHub Repository

A dedicated GitHub repository provides access to all the code, datasets, and exercises referenced in this book. The repository is organized into clear sections for easy navigation.

Repository Structure

plaintext

```
llm-engineering/
│
├── code_samples/
│   ├── chapter_1/
│   ├── chapter_2/
│   ├── chapter_3/
│   └── ...
│
├── datasets/
│   ├── sample_dataset.csv
│   ├── text_classification/
│   ├── sentiment_analysis/
│   └── ...
│
├── exercises/
│   ├── beginner/
│   ├── intermediate/
│   └── advanced/
│
├── README.md
```

└── requirements.txt

How to Access the Repository

1. Visit the GitHub repository at:

2. Clone the repository locally:

bash

```
git clone https://github.com/username/llm-engineering.git
```

3. Install the required dependencies:

bash

```
pip install -r requirements.txt
```

4. Navigate through the sections to explore sample code, datasets, and exercises.

Examples Included in the Repository

1. **Sample Code**:

   o Full implementations of fine-tuning, deployment, and optimization techniques.

   o Example: LoRA-based fine-tuning, quantized inference pipelines.

2. **Datasets**:

   o Preprocessed datasets for sentiment analysis, summarization, and classification tasks.

3. **Exercises**:

   o Beginner to advanced-level challenges with solutions.

---

www.ingramcontent.com/pod-product-compliance
Lightning Source LLC
LaVergne TN
LVHW081756050326
832903LV00027B/1970